Street Kid

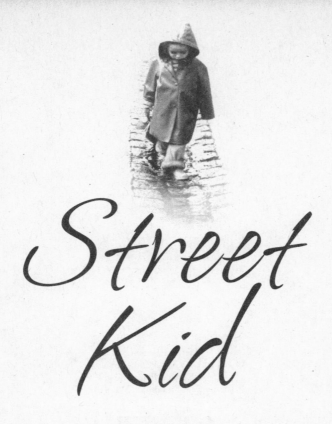

Street Kid

One Child's Desperate Fight for Survival

JUDY WESTWATER

With Wanda Carter

HarperElement
An Imprint of HarperCollins*Publishers*
77–85 Fulham Palace Road
Hammersmith, London W6 8JB

and *HarperElement* are trademarks of
HarperCollins*Publishers* Limited

Published by HarperElement 2006

ISBN 978-1-61664-207-5

FOR MY TREASURED FAMILY

My beloved children Jude, David, Carrie and Erin
and all my beautiful grandchildren

Acknowledgements

I would like to express my deep and sincere thanks to all who have made this book possible.

Special thanks to my dear friend Shaun McKenna, for his unfailing support and steadfast encouragement.

My deep gratitude to John Peel for his absolute faith in my story, and also to Annette Wells and all the research team at BBC Radio 4's *Home Truths*.

A huge thank you to everyone at HarperElement for all their enthusiasm and hard work: Belinda Budge, Carole Tonkinson, Liz Dawson and Sarah Squire. A special hug for Susanna Abbott, my editorial director, for her sensitivity, warm friendship and invaluable advice.

For their caring support, many thanks to fellow inmates at St Josephs Marie Fielding and Tony Toole.

Big hugs to ace photographer Peter Weaver, my special brother-in-law, for his artistic eye, care and support.

My grateful thanks to Virgin Atlantic Airways for their fantastic help and support throughout the years, and to all the co-ordinators in the Sponsorship and Charity Department for their kindness and understanding.

And finally, my sincere thanks and great appreciation goes to Wanda Carter, a very special friend. Her infectious enthusiasm, faith and dedicated belief in *Street Kid* from the beginning led the way and 'twas her guiding hand in mine that made it all possible. Thank you.

I used to wake up icy and wet. I still remember the terrible cold. We'd cuddle together in one bed as soon as it got dark, as there was no light or heat in the house, and I suppose I must have wet myself most nights. I have another memory too, of being alone in the dark, standing halfway down the stairs. I think I must have been looking for somebody but there was nowhere to go in the dark and you couldn't ask for anything because there was nobody there. It was pitch black at the bottom of the stairs so I didn't dare go any further but I couldn't see anything at the top either. I was stuck there, in the freezing, scary darkness and there was nowhere to go and I knew that it was no use crying because no-one would come. I suppose in the end I must have fallen asleep on the step but I don't remember.

Chapter One

I was two when Mum and Dad deserted us, leaving Mary, Dora, and me alone in the house for seven weeks without food, light or coal for the fire.

I was born in Cheshire in 1945 and although the war had ended that year, it had been a battleground in our house whenever my parents were together. When my dad wasn't working in a factory he was dressed up in a herringbone tweed suit preaching at local spiritualist church gatherings. It was only when my mother married him that she realised what a nasty piece of work he really was but she still managed to have three kids with Dad before she decided she'd be better off with her Irish boyfriend, Paddy.

When Mum ran off she took with her our identity cards and allowance books. She must have thought that my father would see to it that Mary, Dora and I were fed and clothed but all he did when he realised he was saddled with us was ask our next door neighbour, Mrs Herring, to look in on us every so often and check we were okay. He said he'd be back the next weekend but he didn't keep his promise.

So that was how the three of us came to be left in the house alone.

Mary was seven, and the oldest. I reckon that as soon as I was born, I knew better than to cry for my mother: it was always Mary who'd looked after me and Dora. Mrs Herring looked in on us now and then, letting us have whatever scraps she could spare; but it was Mary that kept us going. She must have longed for a mother's care herself, especially when she had to go to school in such a terrible state. All the teachers were appalled that she was so dirty, and they'd often have her up in front of all the class to tell her off.

One day it got so bad for Mary that she dragged our tin bath into the living room, put it in front of the fireplace, and started filling it with cold water. She pulled me up from the hearth, where I was eating ashes, and said, 'Come on, we've got to get you dressed. We've got to go and look for Mummy.'

We went out and made our way to the market, which wasn't far from our house. It was cold; my feet were bare; and all the clothes hanging from the stalls were flapping in my face. I kept looking through them to see if I could see my mother.

And Mary kept saying, 'Look for Mummy.'

After seven weeks, Mrs Herring was at the end of her tether. She had only meant to look out for us for a few days. She must have thought, 'Where the heck is their father?' Maybe Dad sent her messages saying he'd be back in a week or something. But the weeks went by and we were in a terrible state. In those days, times were tough but people looked out for each other, and I'm sure Mrs Herring just thought she was doing her best. But at some point she must have realized she had to do something or we'd get really sick. A bitter winter was setting in and we had no money for coal or food. When I touched my hair,

I could feel it was all matted and crusty, and my body was covered in weeping sores that hurt when I lay down.

Mrs Herring contacted the welfare people, who managed to track down my father and served him with a summons. Dad suggested to them that he find someone to look after us in exchange for free lodging at our house, and they agreed with the plan. A homeless couple of drifters called the Epplestones came forward, and the welfare board was satisfied. In the years after the war they could barely keep up with the rising tide of poverty and need, so once our case was closed they didn't bother their heads about us again.

After five months my mother returned home, pregnant and penniless. My dad allowed her back in the house on the understanding that she didn't see Paddy again and had her baby adopted. She agreed.

I don't remember being glad Mum was back or anything like that. You only feel glad or relieved if you have something to compare it with but life with her had always been pretty awful for us. Still, it was better than being in the care of Mrs Epplestone who'd hated having to look after us and shouted a lot. Most of the time, Mary, Dora and I had sat huddled like mice on the old brown couch in the living room, with its springs poking through the cover. But it was when it came to mealtimes that the horror really began. Bowls of porridge were banged down in front of us and when I couldn't eat the nasty, slimy, lumpy stuff, Mrs Epplestone would yank my head back by the hair and force the spoon down my throat until I couldn't breathe. When I choked and gagged she'd hit me across the face.

Mum had no intention of giving up her baby when it arrived and when my Dad discovered that she was keeping her he was furious and came straight over to the house. It was a frosty New Year's Day and Paddy was round, warming himself in front of the fire. He must have come in for a quick one with my mother and to see the new baby. They both got a big shock when the door opened and there was my father. When he walked in and saw them playing happy families, and Paddy's trousers over the chair – in his house – all hell broke loose. The men tore into each other like dogs. My mother was screaming like a banshee, and they were hammering into each other with their fists and breaking up the furniture.

Paddy was a big fellow, much larger than my father, and he'd been a boxer in the army, so he soon got the upper hand. Dad stood there, all bloody with his chest heaving, knowing he'd been beaten and yet burning up with fury and wanting to kill them both. Mum and Paddy looked back at him, confident now that my father had been beaten. My mum told him that they were keeping the baby and that there was nothing he could do about it.

Being told he couldn't do anything made my dad determined to show that he was still boss in his own house. He strode across the room to where we were huddled, boiling with anger, and grabbed me. I hid my face against Mary's chest and clung to her. She and Dora held on tight, screaming at him, 'Leave her alone! Leave her alone!' But they only managed to hang on to me for a few seconds before he peeled their arms away.

I don't think I made much of a sound, but I can still hear Mary and Dora screaming my name as my father dragged me down the street. I can remember my legs not being able to touch the ground: they were just batting the air as Dad took great big strides to get away from the house. I didn't know where we were going or what was going to happen. I'd just seen him fighting Paddy and was terrified that it might be my turn next. I don't know how far I was dragged but it seemed like a long way. I didn't have a coat and felt colder than I'd ever been in my life.

I'd never been separated from my sisters before. The trauma of having been left on our own at such an early age had made us terrified of leaving each other's sides. At night we'd always slept in one bed and during the day we moved about the house like silent triplets or sat on the sofa wrapped in each other's arms. I think we were frightened one of us might disappear. And now I had.

When we arrived at my father's place there was a dark-haired woman sitting at the table. Her face was rigid and, although she didn't say anything, I sensed that she was shocked. I wasn't really aware of much that first evening as I was almost catatonic with fear, but in the days that followed, I realised from the way she treated me that this sharp-faced woman hated me.

Her name was Freda and she'd left her husband and child for my father. He had promised her the moon and now he here he was, walking in with a two-year-old child in tow and telling her that she had to look after me. It wasn't surprising she was bitter. All her dreams of starting a new life in their own little love nest, just the two of them, were shattered in that moment.

Things were only to get worse for Freda. The spiritualist union were tipped off by her husband that she was living in sin with one of their preachers, a man who had deserted his wife and three kids and the scandal was soon splashed over the local papers. My dad and Freda were effectively run out of town and we wandered homeless for weeks. No one wanted anything to do with an adulteress who had left her baby.

Finally, we had a lucky break. A friend of Freda's knew an old couple who needed caretakers for their shop in Patricroft, an old mill town near Manchester. When we went into the shop I thought we'd gone in to buy something. It smelt of sugar and biscuits, and I saw meringues on a shelf by the door. There were newspapers, jars of sweets and cakes, and my stomach gave a rumble as we walked through to the back of the shop. When my father introduced us to the lady behind the counter, she led us through the door behind her and down some stone steps to a room at the back.

Gertie and George Roberts, the owners of the shop, interviewed my dad in the living room of the flat that was to become our home. It had a fireplace and a back door that led out into the yard, a table under the window, a sink in a sort of cubicle, and a tiny two-ring stove.

I'd been cleaned up a bit before the interview, but I expect I must still have looked a sight. My dad was on his best behaviour and laid it on pretty thick, acting the loving family man, trying hard but down on his luck.

'This is my wife, Freda, and that's Judy, our daughter.' I sat on my stool quietly, hearing his lies but not reacting, knowing I'd be severely punished later if I did.

'You see, I was made redundant from the factory and since then we've been struggling to get by.' His shoulders slumped dramatically.

'Oh dear me, you poor things. I know it's been bad for so many just now.' Gertie's face was creased with pity and concern.

'The thing is, I've been trying to do my best for them, but it's been really hard and we've got nowhere to go.'

George looked at his wife and cleared his throat. 'Well, we'd like to help you and you seem like good folk. I know

Gertie would agree with me that we'd like the job to go to a family who really needs it.'

'We're hard workers,' said Dad, 'and we'll do well for you, I promise you that. We never dreamed we'd be lucky enough to find a job and a roof over our heads too.'

I really felt I had a home now, all because of Auntie Gertie and Uncle George. Uncle George looked like Father Christmas – fat, with a white beard and huge rosy cheeks. He used to sit in the chair while Auntie Gertie helped Freda, and I'd stand against his knees by the fire, happy to be feeling so comfy. I don't think he spoke much to me, but I liked it that way.

Auntie Gertie was a big-boned woman who looked rather dour; but she was the gentlest person – never aggressive in any way – and had arms that sort of snuggled you. She also helped Freda a lot in the first weeks. I used to watch her mixing the ice-cream by the door of the shop. She gave me a meringue while I sat there with her, which I ate in little bites. She also took us down the steps into the cellar, where she showed Freda how to use the plunger for the washing and the mangle to wring the water out of the wet clothes.

I still missed my sisters terribly and thought of them a lot, especially before I went to sleep at night. I lay on an old settee in the box room upstairs, wondering if they were thinking about me too, and whether Mary wanted to put her arms around me as much as I longed for her to hold me safe and warm.

After the first couple of weeks, once Freda had got the hang of things, Uncle George and Auntie Gertie hardly came round any more. When their dog, Jessie, died they were completely heartbroken and, without the excuse of a walk, didn't leave their house much. When George and

Gertie were around, Freda minded her behaviour and acted the dutiful wife and mother. But now she had the place
to herself, things really began to change.

My dad soon got a job in a linen factory, where they made
handkerchiefs and eiderdowns. He worked nights as a
security guard and slept during the day. I don't think I
ever saw him, unless it was a Sunday. Freda shut me out in
the yard as soon as the papers were delivered to the shop
in the morning, so I never saw my father come in. And
because he was never around, Freda could be as vicious to
me as she liked.

In the box room where I slept, there were stacks of boxes all round, making it difficult to get undressed. I didn't
have pyjamas or a nightdress, so I wore my vest in bed
and covered myself with a blanket to keep warm. In the
morning, as soon as I heard Freda coming out of her
room, I would get up and put on my dress and cardigan
and go downstairs.

One morning, I came down to find Freda waiting for
me. The paperboy had just arrived and she grabbed my
arm impatiently and took me to the back door.

Pushing me roughly outside she said, 'Sit there. I don't
want you moving.' She pointed to a spot on the paving in
the middle of the yard, gave me a vicious little nudge so
that I almost fell down the steps, then went back inside.

I walked over to the spot she'd pointed at and sat down.
There was nothing to be seen but enclosing grey walls,
and a bucket standing against the door of the outdoor
toilet. I sat on the cold paving stones wondering when
Freda was going to let me in. I remained there for an hour
or so, scared to move in case I'd be punished. I remember
putting my finger in a crack between the paving stones

and moving it along the tiny strip of sand. Then I traced the outline of one of the stones, then another beside it. It wasn't a very interesting game, but I made it last for a long time.

I'd been told to stay put, but, as I wasn't wearing any tights or socks, the cold began to get to me. I needed to move about to keep warm, so I stood up and went over to the steps, looking nervously at the back door. I was curious to see what was over the dividing wall, so I climbed up the steps to look into the next yard. I saw it was almost the same as ours, except for a few plants.

I then tried jumping down the steps, one at a time, then climbing up again. I did this at least twenty times, then got bored of it and sat down and looked at the sky. I watched it for ages. I saw the smoke coming out of the chimneys and the patterns it made, and the pigeons on the roofs, hopping about and sitting hunched up in pairs by the chimney pots.

It was several cold hours before Freda opened the back door.

'Get in,' she said.

She didn't even look at me. It was as if she was letting in the dog.

'Have your tea, then get out of my sight.' She pushed a cheese triangle across the table at me.

Afterwards, I went and sat under the table, which was where I always hid when Freda was around. It had a long cloth, so no one could see I was there. I stayed quiet as a mouse until it was time to go up to bed.

After that, Freda shut me outside in the yard every day. The first time it rained, I ran to the back door and tried to get in, but it was locked. I hadn't known until then that Freda actually locked the door. By the time I'd made it to the privy

9

I was soaked through. I had to shelter in the toilet most of the afternoon, which smelt damp and mouldy, like the cupboard under the sink, and I felt I'd never get warm again.

One day, when it was just starting to spit with rain, our neighbour, Mrs Craddock came out of her house and looked over the wall.

'All by yourself, chicken?' She tutted and cooed, coaxing me over. I approached her cautiously. Mrs Craddock had rollers in her hair and was wearing a flowery pink overall, stretched tight across her enormous bosom.

'Come inside and keep warm.' She scooped me up, lifted me over the dividing wall and put me down in her yard. I saw she was wearing brown tweed slippers with pom-poms on them.

'Let's get you warmed up then.'

She took me by the hand, led me indoors, and sat me down on the sofa by a big fireguard that had washing hanging over it. I was very frightened. I'd been told to stay in the yard.

Mrs Craddock stood at the window watching for Freda, hands on hips, and as soon as she saw her get off the bus she opened the front door. I tried to slip past her but she pushed me back, tucking me behind her, protectively.

I was panicking badly now. *I'm going to be in big trouble. Freda's going to go mad.*

But Mrs Craddock was puffed up with rage and nothing was going to stop her now. She didn't pause to think that I'd be the one getting hurt at the end of it.

'Oi Freda! What do you bloody think you're doing leaving this child in the yard? It was raining for Christ's sake!'

'What the hell's she doing there? Give her back here! And you can take your fat nose out of my bloody business.'

Freda's face looked sharp and pointy as a knife and I thought she was going to go for Mrs Craddock.

'You stupid cow! I don't know how you can stand there. People like you should never be allowed to have kids!'

They went at it hammer and tongs, watched by some of the women from neighbouring houses. Finally, Freda grabbed me and took me with her, slamming the door behind her. She dragged me through the shop and down the steps into the room at the back. I thought she'd beat me senseless, but instead she gave me a couple of slaps and sent me to bed. I think the row with Mrs Craddock had exhausted her. Mrs Craddock never took me in again. But from then on, other people began looking out for me, and occasionally they threw toys over the wall.

One day, there was a thunderstorm and I was feeling frightened. A girl came running over to me. She wasn't wearing a coat and was getting drenched. She looked about eight or nine and had ringlets, which the rain had plastered against her head.

'My mum said to come and fetch you.'

She lifted me over the wall and we ran, hand in hand, through the sheets of rain to her house. Her mum was waiting at the door.

'You poor little thing. You come in and get dry.' She led me into the kitchen and dried me with a towel, fussing over me as she did so.

'I'll make you a cup of cocoa. That'll warm you up. What's your name, poppet?' She was talking to me soothingly as she put some milk and water on the hob.

'Judy,' I whispered.

'And how old are you?'

'Three and a half.'

'Now poppet, I think you'll get warmer if you come into the living room and sit by the fire.' She led the way to the other room, where her two daughters and husband were sitting.

'Tony, this is Judy. She got all wet in the storm,' she said.

'Hello young lady. How would you like to come sit by the fire with me and help me win the pools?' With that, he scooped me onto his knee and let me help him pick out the winning teams with a pin on his football coupon.

It was the first time I'd ever got a glimpse of what family life could be. I bathed in the warmth of it.

Chapter Two

*F*reda never gave me anything to eat or drink in the mornings. Whenever I got thirsty, I'd scoop water from the toilet; but there was nothing I could do to calm the gnawing hunger I felt every day.

It wasn't long before I made my escape from the yard. One day I stood on tiptoe to reach the bolt on the back gate. I pulled on it with all my strength and when it slid back it cut my hand. But it didn't matter to me that it was bleeding because I'd got out. The only worry I had was that now I'd opened the door, I couldn't close it from the other side. But a second later I managed to slip the toe of my sandal underneath and closed it. I felt very proud of myself.

On the other side of the gate I was faced with a high stone wall with a path running along in front of it leading to a small green square with rows of houses backing onto it. As I stood there on the grass, a boy came up to me. He must have been about twelve.

'You alright? Are you lost or something?' I didn't answer, didn't run away either. I just stood there. Then he went away.

From time to time I noticed women coming out of their back doors carrying bags of rubbish over to the low, open-topped bins at each corner of the square. My tummy hurt from hunger and so, as soon as the women were gone, I went over to one of the bins, stood on a brick, and leaned in to hunt for scraps.

The smell was almost overpowering, but I delved down into the damp and greasy rubbish, rummaging through it looking for something edible. I found a promising looking newspaper parcel and unfolded it. Inside there was a handful of potato peelings and some chicken bones. I picked up a bone and sucked on it, tearing off a few tiny strands of meat with my teeth. It tasted good, but didn't satisfy my hunger one bit, so I started on the peelings. They didn't taste nice at all. After eating as many of them as I could stomach, I leaned further over the bin and dug down deeper, looking for other newspaper parcels. I spotted one, and pulled it loose. It contained an old crust of bread and some bacon rind, which I eagerly devoured.

That first time I ventured out of the yard, I didn't go any further than the square behind our houses, but it wasn't long before I was exploring the rest of the neighbourhood. I wandered down the gutters and cobbled alleyways that ran between the rows and rows of back-to-back brick houses. None of them had front gardens or yards and, without a flowerbed or patch of grass to bring colour to the streets, Patricroft was a monotonous place of grey stone and sooty brick. The only things that brought colour to the place were the barges which shipped their cargo along the old canal. I'd stand on the iron bridge and watch them for hours as they made their slow progress through the tar-coloured water, littered with bottles and other bits of rubbish. If anyone came towards me I'd run away and hide.

One day, about three months after we'd moved to Patricroft, and soon after I'd first escaped from the yard, I walked past a gate, through which I could see some grass. Thinking it must be the entrance to a park, I pushed open the gate and went in. I found myself in a large garden, with beds of beautiful flowers planted in patterns. I'd never seen anything so wonderful in my life, and wandered through the garden in the sunshine, hardly aware of time.

After a while, I thought I'd better go home – it must have been mid-afternoon at least, and I was always careful to get back to the yard in good time. But when I looked for the gate I couldn't find it. I began to wander further and then started to panic. I skirted the big, grey stone wall of the building in the centre of the garden, thinking that if I went round it I might find my way back to where I started. Then, as I came round the corner, I was met by a curious sight.

Groups of children in grey uniforms were playing on the grass in little groups. Moving about amongst them was the strangest looking person I'd ever seen. She was wearing a long black dress that flapped as she floated along the grass, and her hair was completely covered with black cloth too. She was gliding along as if on motorized wheels. It was my first sight of a nun.

I watched for about ten minutes, and then a loud clanging noise almost had me jumping out of my skin. One minute it had been quiet and peaceful, the next a huge bell was ringing right above my head. I crouched by the big stone steps, frozen in terror and certain that it was telling everybody where I was. I thought I might have stood on something and set it off.

My fear grew even worse when the groups of children starting coming towards me. They came over to the steps and lined up in pairs. I was crouching down between a shrub and the side of the steps, watching the children as they went up, hand in hand. About ten pairs went by without seeing me, but then I must have made some little movement. My eyes met those of a little girl. It was clear she'd spotted me: she began to tug on the nun's sleeve and said something to her while looking back at me. Then the nun turned and glided over, her big black dress flapping as she came.

'What are you doing here? What is your name?' I knew my name but I couldn't say it. I couldn't speak to her.

'Come with me.' I couldn't move. When someone said 'Come with me' it always meant only one thing. I was certain the nun was going to beat me for being in her garden.

She took my hand and beckoned to the little girl who'd seen me. 'Josephine, I'd like you to take her to the kitchen.' Her tone of voice wasn't particularly warm, but at least I wasn't getting beaten yet.

The girl took my hand and we both went up the steps together. It felt like I was entering a huge mouth as we went through the great doorway. *I'm going to get swallowed*, I thought to myself. We walked through the hall, which smelled of polish, to an enormous kitchen with a long scrubbed wood table in the middle. The only things that brought brightness and colour to the stark room were the copper pans hanging on the walls. Everything else had a sober black and white formality, and even the older girls who were preparing food on tables around the sides of the room in their white dresses looked austere. I was told to sit down and one of the girls brought me a slice of bread and jam, which I devoured hastily, despite my apprehension.

The woman in black came in and began asking me questions again.

'Where do you live? Just tell me your name.'

I looked at her, still unable to speak.

She was huffing and puffing, quite irritated now. She left the room but returned a few minutes later with a group of girls and boys.

'Do any of you know this girl? Have you seen her before?' No one answered.

The nun appeared even more exasperated and turned back to me.

'Come on, we'd better go and see if we can find where you live.'

She took my hand and we went out of the kitchen, back through the hall and out into the sunshine again. We went through a different gate to the one I'd come in by. It was bigger and led onto the main road, with the canal opposite. I told the nun that I knew where we were and made to go; but, to my horror, she kept hold of my hand and began to march me up the street towards the door of the shop.

But I can't go in the front! Don't take me in that way! The panic was rising in a swift tide and washing over me. *Don't take me in that way! I'm supposed to be in the yard!*

The bell tinkled as the nun pushed open the shop door. Freda was looking over from the counter at the back.

'Is this your child?'

Freda said that I was and thanked her very sweetly for bringing me back. Then, as soon as the nun had left, she took me into the back room and closed the dividing door.

'Don't you ever dare go out again.' she screamed. 'Never, ever come in the front, and never ever leave the yard. Do you hear what I'm saying? I'm going to tell your father when he gets back.'

Then she began to lay into me, punching and kicking. She boxed my ears, which she'd done before, only this time the pain was more excruciating. It felt like sharp daggers in my head. I heard a pop and a horrible kind of rushing sound. Freda stopped hitting me and stood, breathing quickly, hands on hips, glaring down at me.

'Get up to your room,' she hissed. 'I don't know why I bother to look after you. You disgust me.'

It was only after I'd got upstairs and crawled under the blanket that I realized I was completely deaf in my right ear.

The next morning Freda recovered her energy and as soon as I'd crept downstairs, heading for my hiding place under the table, she grabbed me and began shouting at me again, calling me a little piece of vermin. She hadn't told my father: I knew she wouldn't, because she would only have got in trouble herself. If he was crossed, he could get extremely vicious; a cold brutality came over him which even Freda, who usually gave as good as she got, was scared of. My dad was always paranoid that someone would pry into his business. He'd come up against the welfare board before, and he didn't want anyone poking their nose into his life now.

Freda grabbed me by the hair and threw me at the back door. She then opened the door and gave me a kick, which sent me tumbling down the steps. I gashed one of my knees against the step, and when I picked myself up at the bottom of the steps I couldn't put any weight on it at first, it was so painful. Then I looked down and saw blood trickling down my leg. I gave a little whimper, but not because of the pain. My dress had got blood on it from the gash and I was suddenly sick to my stomach with terror, knowing that Freda would punish me for getting it dirty. I'd already been beaten by her for losing my bobble hat, and I knew that she'd seize any excuse to beat me.

I hobbled gingerly across the yard to the outside toilet, where I took a square of newspaper from the bundle that hung from a piece of string. Dipping it in the toilet pan, I tried desperately to scrub the blood off my dress with the sodden paper until my arm was shaking, but the blood wouldn't come off.

When Freda let me in later, she looked at my tear-stained face and I knew it made her want to beat the hell out of me. When she saw the state of my dress, stained with blood and spotted with little bits of newspaper, she snatched up the cheese triangle that was sitting on the table and said, 'Right, for that you won't be having any tea, my girl.' As I hadn't been out of the yard that day, I hadn't managed to scavenge anything from the bins, so I was sent to bed with hunger pains gnawing at my insides.

It was only two days later that I once again fell foul of Freda in a big way. It was a sunny day and I was playing in the yard, walking carefully on tiptoe from bar to bar of the iron grate that covered the cellar window. All of a sudden, I slipped and fell, saving myself with my arm. However, my foot had fallen between two of the bars and my leg was dangling in the gap between grate and window. When I tried to pull it out, my knee was in the way; so I tugged and tugged at it, trying to yank it free, becoming more and more panicked that Freda would find me wedged there later when she opened the door. But I couldn't see how I was going to free myself. I was totally trapped and unable to work out why my knee wasn't able to slip back through the way it had gone in. After several minutes of frenzied pulling, my knee got past the bars, but then I found out that my foot in its sandal couldn't get through. I struggled with it until finally my foot came free, but by then my shoe had come off and fallen through the bars.

My leg was cut and bruised and very sore, but I was more worried about my sandal, which was lying below the iron grate, about three feet down. I knew I'd get into terrible trouble if I didn't get it back, so I lay down on the grate and stretched my right arm through the bars. My fingertips didn't even nearly touch it, but I wasn't about to give up. *Come on, you can reach it. Come on!* I couldn't bear to think about what Freda would do if she found I'd lost a shoe. So, again and again, I ground the side of my face down onto the bars in a frenzied attempt to reach my sandal.

When at last I stood up and looked down at my bare foot, I realized that my dress had got dirty from lying on the ground. There was nothing more I could do, so I went over and sat on the steps, where I remained for the next two hours, stiff with fear and awaiting my fate.

When I heard Freda unlock the door, I tried to creep in without catching her eye, but she saw the state of me at once.

'What the hell have you been doing, and where's your shoe?'

I just stared back at her, too terrified to say anything.

She grabbed my arm, pinching it viciously. 'You answer me, damn it! Where's your bloody shoe?'

She yanked my arm and pulled me outside and down the steps. I pointed at the iron grate.

'You little swine. Didn't I tell you not to move? What the hell were you doing throwing your shoe down there?' She poked my forehead with a finger, jabbing it at me so hard my neck snapped back.

Then she went back inside and a minute later I heard her trying to open the cellar window. It was stuck. A moment later, she returned.

'Right, Missie, you lie down and get it!'

I tried to tell her it was no use my trying, but she wasn't listening.

She pushed me down and forced my arm between the bars, though she could see perfectly well that it wasn't nearly long enough to reach the sandal. She put her foot down on my shoulder and pushed. The bars were crushing my chest, making it impossible to breathe.

After a while she dragged me back inside and looked around the room for something long enough to reach the shoe. Finally she stood on a chair, took down the curtain rod, and unhooked the curtain from it. 'Don't you dare move!' she said, taking the rod outside.

A couple of minutes later she came back with the shoe in her left hand. In her right, she held the rod. She whacked me hard across the face with the shoe, making me reel back with the shock of it.

'Get upstairs, damn you,' she snarled. Her eyes were dark slits in her white face.

But as I turned to scramble up the stairs and out of her way, she went for me with the rod, savagely beating the back of my legs. I crumpled to the floor and continued up the stairs on my hands and knees. I felt her black snake-eyes on my back as I turned the corner to my room.

Chapter Three

*A*s Freda's beatings grew worse, so did my health. I was never warm, and felt like I was fighting an endless battle against the cold. Nor do I ever recall feeling full. After a few months, the cheese triangles and meagre scraps I'd taken from the bins took their toll on my body, which grew stick-thin and covered with sores. I slept badly as the abscesses on my back were oozing yellow pus, which made turning over agony.

I'd wake in the morning feeling the sharp pain of hunger, which would persist every minute of the day. Once I found a plug of gum that someone had chewed and stuck to a window sill. It was grey and hard but I was so desperate that I peeled it off and put it in my mouth. I chewed it for a bit but it tasted of nothing; then I swallowed it. Soon afterwards I overheard two boys talking in the street.

'Did you know that if you swallow gum it gets tangled in your lungs?' one of them said. 'And then you can't breathe and you die.'

I could almost feel the horrid, stringy stuff tightening in my chest and had to force myself to breathe in and out. *I can't tell anyone I've eaten it, so I'm going to die*, I thought.

One Sunday evening, a few days after Freda had beaten

me with the curtain rod, Dad was home and he and Freda were having a row downstairs. Freda always wanted me out of the way when my father was around, so she had sent me up to bed early without any tea. I could hear my dad's voice booming under the floorboards of my room, and Freda's tone was as bitter as an acid drop.

I wasn't ready to go to sleep – my hunger pangs wouldn't let me – so I sat on my bed feeling restless and ill. It occurred to me then that there might be some food I could steal in one of the boxes stacked up round the bed, so I started to rummage through them. Then I stood on one of the boxes to get a better look. It tipped a bit as I shifted my weight and suddenly I lost my balance. To stop myself falling, I grabbed instinctively at the pile of boxes next to me. At the top were stacked a few tins of ice-cream wafers and one of these toppled over and fell to the ground with a loud clatter.

My heart almost stopped. Then I heard the voices downstairs go quiet and, a moment later, my father's heavy footsteps on the stairs. I looked down and saw that the tin had come open and broken wafers were scattered everywhere. *Oh no! Don't let them catch me!* I started scrabbling at the wafers on the floor, cramming them into my mouth in a desperate attempt to swallow the evidence.

The door flew open and my father stood there with Freda. They looked at me as though I was no more than a piece of dirt on the floor.

'See what I mean? She doesn't do anything I say,' Freda spat at him. 'Every bloody day I have to put up with this!'

Now she'd got started, it all spilled out – every vindictive little piece of nastiness Freda had been storing up.

'...and she's always stealing ... sneaking around getting the neighbours to stick their noses in ... and dirtying her clothes when she knows I don't have time to run around cleaning up ...'

My dad heard this torrent of poison, all the while looking at me.

'You little brat!' He took a step forward and grabbed my arm, pulling me up. My legs almost buckled under me. 'You want something to eat? I'll give you something to eat.'

Dad dragged me downstairs and sat me on one of the kitchen chairs. Then he took off his braces. I didn't understand at first why he was getting undressed but then he leaned over and stretched the braces around my body, tying me to the chair so I couldn't move my arms. Then he crossed to the kitchen alcove and pulled out a loaf tin and a spoon from a cupboard.

'You want food, do you?' I stared back at him, mutely. 'Answer me! Do you want some food?' I didn't know what to answer, but I knew that whatever I said wouldn't stop him now.

Dad squatted down at the hearth and picked up the coal shovel. He scraped at the back of the fireplace until there was a pile of soot in the grate and then he shoveled it into the loaf tin. I knew now what he was going to do.

'Open up!' He held a spoonful of soot in front of my mouth. I didn't open my mouth at once so he jabbed the spoon between my teeth and forced it in.

My mouth was already dry from the wafers. I tried to swallow, but the soot was clogging the back of my throat. It was bitter and made my eyes stream; then it got into my windpipe and I choked.

My dad forced a second spoon of the stuff into my mouth.

'Eat up, brat! There's plenty to go yet.'

When he couldn't get any more soot in my mouth, my Dad untied me. My chest was heaving violently and my eyes were watery and unable to focus. All I could see through the blur was the terrifying face of my father, ghoulish white with eyes like two black coals fixing me with a cold and psychotic hatred. He reached for his braces and whipped me hard across the head with them before dragging me back up the stairs and flinging me on to my bed.

'I hope that's taught you a lesson.' Then, pointing at the mess on the floor, he said, 'You can clean that up in the morning.'

I lay there, barely able to move my arm to cover myself with the rug. My mouth was sore and bleeding. Sleep came as a blessed relief, but when I woke the next morning the soot still stung my tongue as a terrible reminder of the night before.

Two days later I woke up in the middle of the night feeling very dizzy. The ear that Freda had clouted, bursting my eardrum, was running with pus and my hair was stuck to my face with the fluid. My chest hurt and there was a hot, hard lump on the side of my neck which was making it difficult to breathe. My body was burning up and my throat felt too parched to cry out. It was like being in a bad dream when you try desperately to scream but no sound comes out.

I tried to climb out of bed, but my legs gave way and I fell onto the floor. I crawled across the room in the darkness and when I reached the bedroom door tried to raise myself up to open it, but I didn't have the strength to push myself up with my arms. Freda must have heard me fall out of bed because a moment later I heard her trying to open the door. My body was in the way so she couldn't get in at first. When she managed to push her way in and saw me lying there, I heard her draw in her breath sharply, then run out of the room and down the stairs. She must have gone outside to call an ambulance from the public telephone box in the street because the next thing I knew, a man was lifting me over his shoulder and carrying me down the stairs.

I was taken to a large hospital, where I was put in a steel cot. When the nurses tried to hold me down I struggled like a wildcat, so they had to tie my arms to the bars of the cot with bandages so they could dress my sores. Being tied up meant only one thing to me, so I punched and fought to get away, convinced I was going to get a beating.

Eventually, one of the nurses managed to soothe me. I looked into her soft brown eyes and felt my terror ebbing away.

The next day they took me into surgery and made cuts in my neck and arms and inserted tubes to help drain the big lump below my ear. One of them was threaded all the way down to my stomach. When I came to, I was back in the steel cot, covered from head to toe with bandages, and my arms tied to the bars again. I must have slept through the rest of that day and the next night, but don't remember anything.

On the second night, as I lay in my steel cot, arms tied and face covered, balaclava-like, with bandages, I tried to pierce the darkness with my eyes. I could hear the other children's breathing and occasionally they would moan or say something in their sleep. But there was also another noise, which sounded sinister, as if something ghostly was roaming the room: *swish, swish, swish*, pause, then *swish*,

swish, swish again. I felt like a fly trapped in a web waiting for a hairy, black spider to come and eat me. *Swish, swish, swish.* The noise was very close now, just the other side of my cot. Then I saw a face looking down at me and realized with relief that what I'd heard was simply the nurse's starched uniform swishing against her legs as she patrolled the ward, pausing to check on her patients as she went.

When I was well enough to look around, I saw that I was in a big square room with white walls and a brown lino floor. The sun was streaming in through two tall windows, and along one wall was a row of four steel cots. Facing them were four beds for the older children. In the middle of the ward was a blue table and eight small chairs.

The gentle nurse I remembered from the night they brought me in was talking to me. 'I know you'll like being here between Christening and Lemon.' She pointed at the kids in the cots on either side of me. *What daft names,* I thought. It was only later when another nurse came along to change my dressings that I realized that the children were in fact called Christine and Leonard. It was hard to hear anything clearly with my right ear.

Having my dressings changed was horrible. Only the gentle nurse removed them slowly and carefully. The others all assured me in their no-nonsense way that it was much less painful if they ripped them off really fast.

'There, that wasn't too bad, was it?' I hated that false chirpiness and the fact that they clearly didn't want an answer from me.

My first meal was a bowl of disgusting brown liquid that looked like dirty water. It must have been beef broth, or something similar, but tasted of nothing. The nurse spooned it into my mouth. 'Come on, just a few more mouthfuls and then you can have jelly and custard.' The spoon was very painful as my lips had cuts on them, so she brought a straw and I sucked up the lukewarm liquid with that. I really wanted the jelly and custard so I sucked away at the foul stuff until it was finished.

Four or five times a day a nurse would put each of us little ones on our potties. I'd be lifted out of my cot, still attached to all my tubes. A few days after I'd arrived, the nurse on duty forgot about me half way through her potty rounds. She'd been distracted by one of the other kids, a naughty red-headed boy who was often in trouble, and had forgotten to come back to me. I waited and waited and after an hour or so thought to myself, *I'm just going to have to go.* I wasn't used to asking for help so it didn't occur to me to do so now. I set about trying to get free instead. I wriggled and wriggled my wrists in their bandage ties until one of them came free, then I managed to untie the other. I tried to get out of the cot but my tubes were preventing me, so I took them out of my neck and arms and grabbed hold of the bars to pull myself to my feet. The cot was quite high off the ground, easily taller than me, but that didn't stop me clambering over the side and dropping to the floor.

On wobbly legs, I made my way across the ward to the door I'd seen the older kids use when they needed the toilet. I was sitting there when I heard a huge commotion, a high-pitched raised voice and then a loud click-clack of shoes on the floor. A moment later, my door was flung open and the duty nurse stood there, extremely furious.

'What are you doing, you silly, silly girl. Don't you know you might have *died*?'

I stared back at her, feeling shocked. *I could have died?* It was only at that moment that I realized how severe my injuries had been.

Later that day, a group of people walked into the ward. As they approached my cot, I realized with a sickening jolt that one of them was my father. He was a head taller than the rest and as our eyes met I felt quite breathless with fear. He fixed me with a look which said, *If you so much as utter one word I'll kill you.* Stiffly, he walked over to my bed, accompanied by my doctor, two nurses and a man and woman wearing dark suits. My favourite nurse slid the side of my cot down, untied my hands from the bars and started gently removing the bandages from my head.

Sensing my alarm, she spoke to me soothingly. 'Don't worry, pet. We're just going to have a little look and see how you're doing.'

The other nurse, who was wearing a dark-blue uniform and cap, then spoke. 'Judy, can you tell us how your head and face got hurt.' I shot a nervous look at my father and when I saw his cold grey eyes boring into me, I shut my mouth tight.

Then the man with white hair took a step closer. 'Do you remember how you hurt your legs, Judy. What happened?'

I shrank back from him and when I didn't speak, the man turned to the doctor and said, 'Can she hear me?'

The doctor then came closer and bent his head down. 'Can you remember anything at all, anything about how you got hurt?' I pressed my lips together and shook my head.

At that, my father stepped in, looking like he'd had well enough. 'How many times do I have to tell you?' he said. 'She rode her bike down the hill and crashed into the school railings.'

I couldn't tell the others what I knew: that the school wasn't down a hill, and that I didn't have a bicycle. But I sensed that the people round my bed didn't believe his story anyway.

The white-haired man spoke again, this time to my father. 'Mr Richardson, I'm afraid that during our investigations your daughter will have to stay here in hospital.' My father stiffened a little but didn't say anything.

Then it was over and they turned to go. My favourite nurse stayed with me and gently put my bandages back and tied my hands again. 'You'll see, Judy. We'll have you as good as new in no time,' she said with a smile.

Other than my dad, I didn't have any visitors for a couple of weeks. Every day, after lunch, there was a queue of people waiting to be let into the ward to visit the kids. We could see them through the window that separated our room from the corridor. They stood there making faces and blowing kisses through the glass. I remember Leonard's family coming to visit him in the second week. When he spied his parents he stood up in his cot, calling out and waving at them with both hands. Then his mum and dad came in and they swooped Leonard up and gave him a big cuddle. Later, when they'd gone, Leonard showed me two oranges they'd given him, holding them through the bars of his cot. I wished I could have had one.

Although I wasn't really expecting anybody to come and see me, I still scanned the queue every day to see if I had any visitors. I'd pretty much given up when one day I saw Uncle George and Auntie Gertie smiling and waving at me through the glass. I felt so warm and happy, it was as if the sun had suddenly poked its head out from between the clouds. I beamed back at them from my cot. By then, my bandages had been taken off so I could sit up.

'How's my little injun?' George asked, having settled himself on a chair next to my cot. 'Feeling better?'

I told him that I was. Then Auntie Gertie leaned forward. 'You've got a bit of something on your cheek, poppet.' I'd only recently finished lunch. 'Here, spit on this.' She held out a hanky and I spat on it and she rubbed at my face. 'There, all clean now,' she said.

They didn't stay long and when I saw Uncle George stirring in his chair and glancing at his watch I turned to Auntie Gertie. 'Can I go home with you?' I asked. 'Please!'

'No chuck, not yet. You have to stay here a bit longer.' She stroked my hand. I saw a look pass between her and George and I knew that my question had upset them both. Feeling too old and powerless to do anything made them feel unnerved and I didn't think they'd come again to visit. The thought of me, small and vulnerable, in my hospital cot pleading for a home would, I sensed, become a painful memory that they'd want to push away.

When they left, they blew kisses until they were out of sight. I had an immediate pang of homesickness when they left, but later on I felt comforted by their visit. I'd been sensitive to the fact that the other kids had been wondering what was so wrong with me that no one cared enough to come. Now I'd shown them that I did have friends after all.

I must have been in hospital another week before Auntie Gertie and Uncle George came again. This time it was to take me home. As I sat on one of the little blue chairs in the ward, I wondered where I would be taken. I hoped I might be going back to the Roberts' house, but instead we went to the shop. I was relieved that there was no sign of Freda or my father when we got there; and, as the flat was empty, Uncle George and Auntie Gertie stayed over that night to look after me.

My father and Freda came back late in the afternoon the next day. I slipped quickly to my room and from there heard the row raging downstairs. The Roberts were really angry and I could pick out almost everything the four of them were saying.

'We've been horribly deceived by you,' Uncle George was saying. 'We thought you were a trustworthy pair but you're wicked, just wicked.'

'Oh, and I suppose you know everything,' Freda spat at him. 'Mrs Craddock makes bloody sure of that.'

'It wasn't just her, Freda.' It was Auntie Gertie's turn. 'Your fancy man's wife came round to ours and told us every last detail. That poor little kiddie.'

My heart turned to ice at Auntie Gertie's words and my thoughts were spinning round and round, out of control. *Mum came. She knew I was here. Why didn't she take me home with her?* I felt my heart breaking. *Mum, you must have known how bad it was with him. Why didn't you save me from them? Don't you care for me at all?*

Over the next couple of days, a stream of serious-looking visitors came to the house. From under the table I could see men with polished brown shoes and pinstriped trousers pacing the living room, and ladies with court shoes and nylon stockings sitting with their legs crossed, gloves and handbags placed close to their heels. They asked my dad and Freda a lot of questions in serious-sounding voices. At some point, Mrs Craddock was called in for her pennyworth. She used the 'chicken' word a lot and clucked her tongue in disgust as she reported how badly Freda had treated me.

The next thing I remember, I was on my own with Auntie Gertie and she was putting on my shoes and cardigan. The flat was quite empty. My dad and Freda had gone.

The bell sounded at the shop door. 'Here she is,' said Auntie Gertie, taking my hand and ushering me through the shop. A young nun was standing just inside the door. 'Now Judy, you be a good girl and go with this nice lady.' She gave me a little hug and patted my back. It never occurred to me that this was a final goodbye and that I wouldn't be coming back.

Chapter Four

I'd been many times to the gardens of St Joseph's Orphanage. The flowers and trees kept on drawing me back. After a while, the nuns had got used to seeing me there. I never came close and they never bothered me.

I hadn't been inside the big, grey stone building since that first time. It still scared me. Now, as the nun led me through the polished hall, I wondered if I was going to be given bread and jam again. Instead, I was put in a large room and told to stay there and play. I didn't understand what I was meant to do: I'd never been told to play before. I wanted to go back to the shop and hide under my table in the kitchen. Instead, I crawled into a gap between a bookcase and a piano and hid away there.

It wasn't long before a bell rang. The bell had always been my signal to return to the yard so I jumped up, ready to flee. But before I could do so, the young nun came back.

I tried to wriggle past her, but she took me firmly by the hand.

'You're to stay here now, Judith. At the orphanage.'

The nun then led me firmly by the hand down a long corridor to a huge echoey hall. It was full of children, all making their way to long tables laid with cutlery and glasses, jugs of water, and plates of bread. I was taken to a seat at one of the tables. There was another nun at the head of the table standing behind her chair, hands clasped in front of her. I didn't know what I was meant to do, so I sat down. Seeing the plate of bread, and being used to scavenging for any food I could lay my hands on, I reached over and snatched a slice, hastily stuffing it into my mouth.

I felt a hand yank me up by the back of my collar. 'That is *not* how you behave here, Judith.' The nun looked at me, sternly. 'And the rest of you, be quiet.' At that, all heads ducked down, eyes lowered.

I stood up, instinctively realizing that I'd better copy the other children. Then a much older nun spoke from the table at the top of the room.

'For what we are about to receive, may the Lord make us truly thankful.'

There was a murmured 'Amen' before everyone drew back their chairs and sat down. I did the same. Some older girls then brought bowls of stew and potatoes to the tables. They ladled it onto plates and I waited until the nun at the head of my table raised her fork to her mouth before I dared move. I had never used cutlery before so I dug in with my fingers, stuffing the stew and potatoes in my mouth. The other children stared.

'Judith, you will *not* behave like that here,' she said. 'It's certainly not the way to show our Lord how grateful you are.'

I didn't know what a lord was, or what grateful meant.

After dinner, I was taken to the nursery by the nun who'd brought me back from the shop. The room was white and bare except for twenty cots standing against the walls. She took me over to one of them.

'That's your bed, Judith.' She handed me a nighty. 'Now, get undressed.'

I did as I was told and the nun took my clothes away and brought me some others from a cupboard at the end of the room, putting them on the chair beside my cot. She waited while I got under the covers and then left the room without a word. I hunkered down so that only the top of my head showed above the covers. I wrapped my own arms around me for comfort, imagining they were Mary's, and my breathing slowly steadied until finally I fell asleep.

The next morning, the nun came in at first light and I got dressed with the others while she put the little kids on their potties, five of them in a row. I was confused by the clothes the nun had put out for me, having no idea in what order to put them on. There was a huge pair of woolly pants with a pocket in the front, then something that was a bit like a vest with buttons. I watched another girl and copied her, putting a checked blouse on top of that, followed by a blue pinafore.

The rest of the day seemed to pass in a blur of bells and corridors, and nuns giving me instructions that I couldn't understand. I didn't know how to play with other kids and felt uncomfortable being near them. I was little more than a wild animal, used to fending for myself alone, and the orphanage was a very frightening place to me. Here, you weren't allowed to act alone; you were always part of a large group of children. The nuns only knew how to herd the flock, and shepherding was at the very core of their belief system. From the first, I was both a threat and a challenge to them. A feral, alert-eyed, lone wolf, snatching food and hiding away.

In the playroom, the nun couldn't work out why I crouched in the corner alone all the time and was frustrated that I wasn't playing with the other kids. She kept dragging me out of my hole, saying, 'Will you sit down and play.' But I didn't understand what she was saying. I only knew how to scurry and scavenge, and hide from strangers in my hole.

After supper in the evening, three of the older girls took us to the washrooms. We all got undressed and stood there naked and shivering before being lifted into an enormous bath. I was almost panting with fear at being handled by the girls and having to sit naked with five other children and fought like a wildcat, trying to get away. I couldn't see over the sides of the bath at all. When one of the big girls got a flannel, rubbed it on a giant green block of soap, and started to scrub me all over I panicked when the soap got in my eyes and mouth.

The nun's at St Josephs were an order of Franciscan missionaries who staunchly upheld their vows of poverty, chastity, and obedience. They believed they were setting us on the divine path and controlling our baser instincts when they punished us. They didn't have any understanding of the psychological trauma feral children face, and so, to them, my behaviour was seen as deliberate disobedience; my habitual silence, insolence; and my fierce independence, obstinacy.

In the years immediately after the war, orphanages were spilling over with children and the nuns were needed at home to look after them. Many no doubt felt bitter that their dreams of travelling to a distant land as missionaries hadn't come to anything, and perhaps that made them act more harshly towards us.

About five months after I'd arrived at St Joseph's, I was

moved out of the nursery. By now I was used to my cot and the playroom and moving into the Juniors was a whole new challenge. We had to go to school and attend chapel three times a day, and there was a tough set of routines to learn.

It was an icy January day, four months before my fifth birthday, when I was first taken up to the girl's dormitory. I wasn't prepared for the sheer scale of the room. There had been only twenty of us in the nursery, but this room must have had at least a hundred beds. Each was just a chair apart from the next, and instead of the white eider-downs we'd had in the nursery there were tough wool blankets. On closer inspection, I realized that my blanket was in fact an army greatcoat. There were no toys on the beds, nothing at all to distinguish one from the other. Further along, some of the beds had curtains round them. I later discovered that these were for the older girls. At the far end of the room was the 'cell' where the nun on duty slept.

That first night I felt small and lonely under my army greatcoat. I could hear the little blonde girl in the next bed crying. I lay there looking at the stars – tiny pinpricks of twinkling light in friendly little groups – through the window and wondered if I belonged up there in the sky with them, if they were my real family, and if they were watching over me. Then my thoughts turned to my mum and sisters and I wished I had Mary and Dora here beside me, one on each side, holding me safe.

When morning came, I didn't feel a whole lot better. From the moment I opened my eyes, it was a mad rush and, as hard as I tried, I couldn't keep up with the others. First there was chapel, then breakfast and chores. After that, everyone gathered in the hall and started lining up in a crocodile. Each girl was with a partner. I stood on my own, awkwardly, panicking slightly. Then Sister Cecilia came over.

'Don't just stand there, my girl, you're holding everybody up.' She beckoned to one of the other girls. 'Mary, come over here and line up beside Judith.' The girl came over to stand next to me. She waited until the last minute before putting her hand in mine. I didn't like having to stand with her either; I always felt much safer on my own.

Out in the street, we walked past the alleyway that led to the yard in which I'd spent so many long days. I felt almost homesick for it now.

'Hey, scaredy-cat!' It was the girl behind me. *Oh no, she means me.* I didn't turn round.

A foot deliberately trod down the back of my sandal so that I tripped forward. 'Hey, scaredy-cat!' I turned this time to see the two girls behind me smirking. 'What's the matter, can't you walk proper?'

I didn't react, but just pulled my sandal back on my foot.

I was feeling frayed to the point of tears by the time we arrived in the playground of the big red-brick school. Every few steps, the girl behind me had trodden on the back of my sandal, tripping me up. I stood there and our crocodile of kids seemed to dissolve all of a sudden, leaving me alone in the playground. I ran to the door I'd seen the crowd of kids disappearing through and made my way after them. Everybody else seemed to know exactly where they were going.

I didn't think to ask anyone where to go. Instead I wandered the corridors until I found myself a classroom. I saw an empty desk and sat down at it. So far so good. At least I hadn't had to ask anybody for help.

'What are you doing here?' The teacher had stopped

what she was doing and was looking at me.

'I've come to school,' I whispered.

'You're in the wrong class,' she said. 'You'd better come with me.'

I followed her, feeling thirty pairs of eyes on my back.

There was a certain comfort in having my own wooden desk and the teacher was nicer to us than the nuns. But I still didn't have a clue what I was meant to be doing, which book I was meant to be using, how to sharpen my broken pencil, or what to do when it was break time. I felt horribly confused.

At lunch time, when we were due to go back to the orphanage, I panicked again.

Where are the St Joseph's kids? I can't remember what they look like. What if they leave me behind?

Then I recognized the pinched-looking girl I'd walked to school with in the otherwise unfamiliar sea of faces, and went over to her. I felt completely exhausted, but knew I had to walk back, kneel in chapel, eat dinner, and do my chores before being allowed to go to bed. It seemed like the most interminable day of my life.

Things began to get a little better as I became used to the daily routine; and at school, over the following months, I was taught how to read. It made a wonderful difference to me, being able to read books in the girls' room in the afternoon and after supper. It became a precious way of escaping and I lapped up any stories of rebellious heroes I could lay my hands on, such as Richmal Crompton's William Brown.

Although I eventually got the hang of them, however, I hated the orphanage rules and never ceased trying to act independently – always the lone wolf. That often got me into trouble with the nuns, especially Sister Bridget, who was a bitter woman and often very cruel.

Every item of clothing had to be put on the chair beside our beds in a certain way, with our cardigans neatly wrapped round the back. If I got so much as the smallest detail wrong I would be hit with Sister Bridget's cane. Then there were the kitchen duties: washing and putting away the dishes, laying the table, peeling the vegetables, sweeping the floor; and the cleaning of the bathroom and toilets. If you so much as put a spoon back in a kitchen drawer the wrong way round you'd be for it. At five years old, it was impossible to get every tiny thing right.

Many of the rules at St Joseph's seemed pointless. When I heard Sister Bridget locking the door to the toilets outside in the corridor, after we'd gone to bed, I thought, *What on earth is the point of that? What if someone needs to go to the toilet in the middle of the night?*

One morning, Sister Bridget heard one of the new girls in our dormitory crying. She went over to her, said something, then stripped the sheet and blanket from her bed.

'Look at this wet bed!' she said. 'There's only one way to make disobedient little girls learn the rules. Hold out your hand.' She took a small cane out of her habit and whacked the girl's hand.

As soon as Sister Bridget had left the room, a couple of the older girls came over to comfort the girl.

'Don't worry. If it happens again we'll nick you another sheet from the cupboard,' one of them said, kindly. 'We can smuggle the wet one out under our clothes and dump it in the canal. We've done it before!' This produced a trembling smile from the girl.

'In the boy's dormitory they do it in their boots and tip it out of the window!' the older girl's friend said.

Something made me rejoice in this piece of rebellion. It was refreshing to find that not everybody obeyed the nuns like sheep. I resolved then never to let them beat me down. I sensed that a child could easily lose the sense of who they were in a place like this.

Chapter Five

Mealtimes would often be difficult at the orphanage. Sister Bridget always broke out in a rash of irritation with me at my refusal to eat anything milky and slimy, a hatred which must have stemmed from Mrs Epplestone's force-feeding me porridge. One lunchtime, I sat with my bowl of rice pudding in front of me, nervously moving it around with my spoon. I'd tried to get some of it down, but it was no good. Every time I put some in my mouth I began to retch, so I'd had to give up. Sister Bridget was sitting next to me, watching me like a hawk.

'Judith, will you stop this nonsense this minute,' she said. 'I won't have you wasting the good Lord's food.'

I tried again but couldn't help gagging.

'Eat it now! We will *not* have waste here.'

She watched me a moment then snatched the spoon out of my hand. 'Open your mouth!'

She shoved the spoon in my mouth. I felt immediate and violent panic and had an instant and terrifying flashback to the time Mrs Epplestone had held my head back by the hair and almost suffocated me shovelling porridge down my throat.

I began to choke violently, my eyes streaming. Then I gave one mighty heave and threw up all over Sister Bridget's arm. There was a moment of absolute quiet in the hall. You could have heard a pin drop. The children sat, frozen in horror. Then Sister Bridget stood up sharply, breaking the silence, and grabbed me by the hair.

'Look what you've done, you filthy child!' Her voice was almost a scream. 'What have you to say?'

I had absolutely no idea what I had to say and couldn't speak anyway as I was still gasping for air.

Sister Bridget then repeated, 'What are you going to say?' and tugged my hair.

I shook my head and this seemed to make her anger boil over even more.

'Grateful!' she shouted. 'That's what you must say, "I must be grateful."'

She then turned on the other kids. 'Why can't any of you ever be *grateful*?'

With that, Sister Bridget dragged me out of the room by my hair and down the corridor to the chapel.

'You'll stay there until bedtime,' she said. 'And you'd better ask God's forgiveness. He doesn't like ungrateful little girls.'

I was left alone in the cold, musty chapel with its dark pews and scary painting of Christ, pale and bloody on the cross, eyes rolling back in his head. I sat there waiting for a thunderbolt to strike me.

After this, I was desperate to get out of the orphanage. I longed to visit the shop. In my imaginings, Auntie Gertie would be at the counter, or stirring the ice cream, when I came in and would look up and smile. Then she'd wrap her comfortable arms around me and call me her poppet.

Two days later, as soon as lunch was finished, I slipped out of the orphanage grounds. I felt I could breathe again. But when I entered the shop, that good feeling drained away. There was no Auntie Gertie smiling a welcome. Instead, a strange woman I'd never seen before was behind the counter. I stood for a moment, staring at her. Then she said 'Yes?'

I turned and ran out of the shop and down the street. As I slipped through the gate of the orphanage grounds, I felt even more lost and hopeless than before.

There was a group of us at St Joseph's who were known as the 'forgotten' children. We were the ones nobody ever came to visit, and on those Sundays that were visiting days it was particularly hard for us. Those kids with parents or relations who came to take them out for the day were in a fever of excitement for days beforehand. After chapel, they'd go and sit bolt upright in the visitor's room, washed and scrubbed and smart as new pins in their Sunday best.

Some of the women who visited in their flowery dresses came with soldiers in uniform. There was a lot of laughing and perfume and kissing and then, as the room emptied out through the morning, there was a sad hour or so when one or two kids usually remained, uncollected, the excitement having leaked out of them bit by bit. It was worse for them; at least us forgotten kids weren't expecting anyone, so our hopes hadn't been raised and dashed cruelly in that way.

In my second year at St Joseph's I got to know a boy called Tony. He was a forgotten kid like me, but his mum must have sent the odd message to St Joseph's because on the day I first spoke to him he was sitting on the steps outside, waiting for his mother to arrive. It was nearly teatime when I saw him there in his Sunday best, trying to look unconcerned. It was clear to everyone that his mum wasn't going to come that day, but Tony wasn't going to give up.

I went and sat next to him. I didn't normally choose to go near the other kids, preferring to keep a wary distance. But now I felt an urge to comfort the boy which was strong enough to override my natural fear of people.

'What are you doing?' I asked. I knew the answer, but couldn't think of anything else to say.

'Waiting for me Mam.' Nothing else was said but I sat there for a while with him.

Tony and I didn't have much to do with each other at St Joseph's as the boys and girls were separated at all times, but we played with each other when we were sent away on our summer holiday, and delighted in inventing stories in which the nuns had their comeuppance and the kids were the heroes.

Every August, the orphanage children would be taken for a two-week holiday to Freshfields, near Southport. It was a college connected to the Order and was situated very close to the beach. You could see the sandhills from the grounds.

The rules were much more relaxed at Freshfields and boys and girls were allowed to mix with each other. It was there that Tony and I played hide-and-seek in the dunes and jumped in the water to see who could make the biggest splash.

Tony was a rebel, which I think is what drew me to him. He often tried to escape the orphanage and would be brought back in a taxi by one of the nuns. He knew everything that went on at the orphanage. What we spoke about most that second summer at St Joseph's was the Child Migration Scheme.

One of the most devastating things to happen to many children in Catholic care homes in the 1950s was the migration scheme to Australia. The British Government had decided to send children of 'good British stock' to populate the country, and the Catholic orphanages were major players in the scheme. It all sounded very exciting to us, but we didn't know that many children were being sent off without their parents' permission; some of them were even told their parents were dead when they couldn't be found.

A couple of weeks before our Freshfields holiday, a man had visited the orphanage to tell us about the migration scheme. He set up a projector in the girls' room and showed us slides. He made the whole thing sound like a wonderful adventure.

'You'll have loving parents there,' he assured us. 'And you'll go on a big ship, and have lots to eat. You'll live on great big farms and you'll have a wonderful time. It's always sunny in Australia.'

Tony was sceptical. He knew much more than I did about what was really going on. I'd seen children lining up to have their medicals outside the sick bay before leaving on a coach; but Tony had actually been down to the Liverpool docks and seen the kids being herded onto the boat.

'They allowed some of us to go to wave them off,' he told me as we sat in the lee of a sand dune, sheltering from the wind. 'They were all lined up and there was a man in a uniform at the bottom of the gangway, checking them all off on his list. And there was a black kid he wouldn't take.'

'And what happened then?'

'Well, the kid was pushed back with us and another one taken from our lot who'd just come along to wave good-bye. Glad it wasn't me.'

'I think it would be fun to go,' I said. 'At least you'd be getting out of St Joseph's.'

My wish nearly came true. I was on the list to go to Australia, being one of the forgotten kids. However, Father Gary, our chaplin, was sent out to find as many parents as he could and managed to track down my mum and dad. My father, rather than run the risk of my mother taking me back, and, still locked in his stubborn need to revenge himself on her in any way that he could, said he was now in a position to look after me, that he was getting married to Freda and that they were emigrating to Australia. He'd have a stable home for me now, he assured the authorities.

The next thing I knew, Sister Cecilia had sought me out just before bed one night. She told me that I was to be sent back to my father the next day.

'You're a fortunate girl, Judith,' she said. 'Not many of the children here have a parent who is willing to take them back. You'd better thank the Lord Jesus in your prayers tonight.'

I nearly fainted with shock. *But they hurt me. How could you send me back?*

Sister Cecilia ignored my stricken face. 'You'll be going to Australia and your father's getting married. You're a lucky girl.'

I didn't know where Australia was; I didn't have a clue. But I knew Freda, and I knew him.

In bed that night, the terrifying truth really started to sink in, and I couldn't sleep a wink. I thought of the orphanage as my home now. Although I'd had some horrible times there, I knew the routines – what stairs to go up, what door to go out of – and was used to life at St Joseph's. Now I was being told, 'Off you go, we're done with you here.'

I feel like one of the jigsaw pieces in the playroom that's got into the wrong box; that doesn't fit into any picture.

The next morning I waited, tired and listless, with my bag. Sister Cecilia had brought me the things Auntie Gertie had packed for me three years ago. It felt strange to see my pink dress and shoes again. I didn't suppose they'd fit now. There was also a teddy bear I'd never seen before. It had a little card tied to it and I saw that it was from Mrs Craddock. She must have given it to Auntie Gertie to give to me, but the nuns didn't allow any children to have their own toys so had put it away. Susie, as I christened her, was instantly my most treasured possession.

A young woman I'd never seen before arrived to take me away. She wore a camel-coloured coat with a belt and a pair of red shoes. She must have been a social worker. We sat on the top deck of the bus. I was fidgeting and biting my lip with nerves.

'Will you sit still, child!' she said to me impatiently. I tried to stop wriggling my legs but carried on chewing my lip.

I had no idea how far we were going or where my father and Freda lived now, but our bus journey only lasted about ten minutes. When we got off, the place looked very bleak. We set off across a bombed-out piece of land, which I later learned was called 'the Croft', in the direction of a row of terraced houses. The street had big cobblestones and the social worker had difficulty walking across them in her red shoes. I saw that some of the houses were missing from the row, and there were heaps of rubble which hadn't yet been cleared up. We stopped outside a small two-up, two-down house on the end of the row with a green gas lamp outside it.

The woman knocked on the front door. My father opened it and she pushed me in ahead of her. She was obviously impatient to get away.

'Here's your daughter, then. Let us know if you have any difficulties.'

My father thanked her and she left. Then he turned to me. My reaction was instantaneous – a crippling fear that made my knees almost buckle under me. Nothing, I realized, had changed and, although three years had gone by, I felt no less afraid of my dad than when I was four years old. The old trauma surfaced so fast as I stood there in the hall that I shrunk away from him, filled with horror that I should be having to share a house again with this dark figure who'd inhabited my every nightmare like a malevolent ghoul.

'Freda's through there in the kitchen. Go and say hello.'

On shaky legs I walked into the front room and put down my bag. I walked through the room feeling as if I was on my way to the gallows, such was my trepidation at meeting Freda again. She had managed to create a respectable family room, complete with Singer sewing machine and piano, but I knew that she would be just the same vicious snake as she always had been. I walked through to the back kitchen where I could hear her at work.

Freda was washing dishes at a square, brown pot-like sink and she turned when she heard my footsteps on the flagstone floor.

'So, you're here. Grown a bit, I see,' she eyed me critically. 'You'd better go up and put your bag in your room.'

Upstairs there were two more rooms. Freda led me to the one on the left, containing a single bed with an eiderdown, which was a change from my old sofa and blanket at Patricroft. There wasn't a light in the room, just a table, on which had been put a meccano set.

'You are never, ever to touch that,' Freda told me in a harsh, emotionless voice. The toy, I knew, was the one memento she had of the son she'd deserted.

'And don't think for a moment that I want you here. You're a lying, thieving little sneak and always will be.'

Chapter Six

The next morning, Freda showed me what my duties were. She took a cold and savage pleasure in pointing out every little thing that needed to be done, jabbing her bony finger at a hospital corner on her bed-clothes, or a crevice in the iron range that needed to be cleaned just so. She had her other hand on her hip and spoke to me as if I was an idiot.

So began my new life as a seven-year-old slave in the town of Hulme.

The next morning, as soon as it was light, I got up, dressed and went downstairs. Freda and my father were still in bed and the house was chill in the grey light of early morning.

First, as instructed by Freda, I emptied the ash dust out of the grate in the kitchen fireplace, then cleaned the fire back and put aside the partially burned pieces of wood to use later. Next, I let myself out of the back door, loaded two buckets with coal from a heap in the yard, and chopped the large logs of wood into smaller pieces with an axe.

I struggled to remember what Freda had told me and kept getting it wrong or would forget something. She'd instructed me how to lay the fire and I knew she wanted the coal positioned in a certain pattern, but I couldn't remember if the smaller pieces should be put on first or the bigger. I felt hot and panicky. If it wasn't just so, I knew that Freda would hit me.

After laying the fire, I scrubbed the hearth, then cleaned the ashes off the mantelpiece. By now, I was exhausted but I still had to lay the kitchen table for breakfast and fill a kettle with water so I could wash up last night's pots and pans.

A week later, black and blue from Freda's beatings, I started at Duke Street School; and then things became even tougher for me, as all my chores had to be done before I left.

Freda had a part-time cleaning job in the flat behind the local newsagents. She wasn't home when I got back from my first day at school. She'd given me a key to let myself in with which I wore around my neck on a string. I soon realized that she didn't like to be there when I was doing all the afternoon chores; so if she wasn't working, she'd be down at Lewis's or Pauldines, Manchester's big department stores, shopping with her friend Madge or having tea round at her house.

I let myself into the house and quickly got to work. I started by sweeping the floor, then washed the lino in the front room with a scrubbing brush and a cloth. Next I went upstairs. I was dreading going into Freda and Dad's room as I felt at any moment that one of them might walk in. I quickly made the bed then hung up any clothes strewn about the room. Lastly, the worst job of all.

I bent down and slid the chamber pot out from under the bed. It was full of urine and, to my disgust, there was excrement there too, the smell of which made me gag.

I carried the heavy pot across the room and down the stairs. A couple of times, on the way to the outdoor toilet, urine slopped over the sides so that, after scrubbing and drying the pot, I had to get a cloth and bucket and wash the stairs too.

My next job was scrubbing the kitchen floor. If Freda so much as noticed one little pool of water left between the uneven flags I'd get a beating. Everything had to be perfect. She'd slapped me across the face the previous week when I'd failed to do up the buttons on her blouse before hanging it up. I didn't even know that was how it was meant to be done, but I knew excuses would be pointless.

Freda also delighted in inspecting every nook and cranny in the range, knowing that it was the hardest job to do well. If she'd been cooking something that had boiled over, like a rice pudding, I had to use wire wool to clean the brown, crispy gunge from the oven and it made my fingers bleed. Once a week, I had to black-lead the range – the previous day it had taken me an hour and a half.

I'd just finished my chores by the time Freda got home. The moment I heard her open the front door and put down her bags, my heart began to pound. I stood hiding behind my bedroom door, hardly daring to breathe and listening with every nerve-end to the sounds she made as she moved around the front room and kitchen inspecting my work.

Then came Freda's steps on the stairs. I heard her walking round her bedroom checking everything. Then she came back out onto the landing outside my door.

Please go downstairs. Please let everything be perfect!

Freda opened my door. 'Get out from behind there!' Her voice was icy. 'You've been lazy again, you idiot girl. Can't you ever do anything right?' Freda's mouth was set in a hard line and her eyes were slits of fury. Snatching the library book I'd been reading, she lunged at me, whacking me across the head with it.

'I'm confiscating this, and maybe then you'll learn.'

Somehow, with an unerring instinct, Freda knew that this would be the worst punishment of all. In taking my book, she took away my one source of escape.

I lay on my bed dry eyed. I could almost feel myself pushing down the emotion I felt and locking it away in a cold, secret box in my chest. However beaten or bullied I was, however great the injustice done to me, I could never speak up to defend myself and I'd never learned to cry. I discovered from the moment I was born that tears would never bring comfort or caresses, only harsh words. And now here I was, seven years old and never daring to speak in case I got hit across the mouth for it.

I lay there in the dusk, watching the gas lamp's greenish glow cast strange shadows on my wall and feeling the cold box in my chest weighing me down, a huge, hard lump that could never be eased by tears.

My father would get up after I'd left for school in the morning, have his breakfast and leave for work. He had a job as a fitter and turner at a company called Three Six Five. He was a vain man, obsessed with maintaining the new veneer of respectability he and Freda had created, and didn't want to be seen coming home in his overalls like the other blue-collar workers. He hated the idea of our neighbours knowing he was a fitter, so he changed into his normal clothes at work before coming home.

One of the things my father obsessed about was having a perfectly polished doorstep. Freda had shown me how to use the donkey stone she'd got in exchange for rags from the rag-and-bone man. It was made of crushed stone, bleach, and cement and was used by all the housewives in our street to scour and colour their doorsteps. 'Doing the step' was another of my daily chores.

First, I'd bring out a bucket of warm water and a cloth and wipe down the doorstep. Then I'd wet the donkey stone, taking off a layer of the chalky stuff with my cloth. The paste was then spread on the step and left to dry. It left a smooth caramelly residue and, with a clean cloth and water, I'd wash around it carefully to make a perfect semi-circle. My father always insisted on a half-moon shape. Everyone else in the street had their step coloured in a square, but he wanted to show he was better than them. It was very hard marking out the semicircle, but I knew Dad would beat me if I didn't do it perfectly.

On my first Saturday in Hulme, I was lying on my bed when I heard the rag-and-bone man outside shouting, 'Any old rags!'

'Judy, get down here now!' Freda's voice made me jump.

I ran downstairs. Freda shoved an old white shirt of my father's, and a few other bits of clothing and rags, into my arms and told me to get a donkey stone.

I went outside into the winter sunshine. A group of kids from the neighbouring houses had collected on the street with their armfuls of rags, twittering with excitement.

The rag-and-bone-man had longish, grizzled hair and was unshaven. His trousers were kept up with string, but his big shire horse didn't look badly fed. He probably wasn't that hard up as he was paid good money for a ton of rags across town at the paper factory.

One by one, the children gave the man their bags of old clothes and he held up a selection of toys they could choose from. One girl with an especially big bundle of rags

was allowed to take a bat with a ball attached by a piece of
elastic. I looked longingly at the bazooka, which I'd seen
the other children blowing into and which made a really
funny buzzy sound. 'So what do you want, love?' the rag-
and-bone man asked me.

I knew what I had to say.

'A donkey stone.'

'Here you are then.' He handed the chalky cream block
to me. I went back indoors, not wanting to stick around
watching the other kids playing with their new toys; but I
could hear the buzzing from their bazookas and the loud
clacks as they flicked their wooden clappers as I walked
back over the cobblestones.

Another chore Freda gave me was humping our tin bath, full
of dirty laundry, down to the wash house. Doing the washing, when no one in our street had hot water or a tub, was
something that took the women most of the day. The wash
house was only a short walk from our terrace, and a crowd
of women would set out in the early morning, dressed in
flowery overalls, hair tidied away in brightly coloured
scarves tied in a knot at the top. In front of them, they'd
be pushing old prams piled up with the week's washing.

Freda used to do the laundry at the wash house, but it
was my responsibility to get it there in the morning before
school. I used to look longingly at the women's prams as I
staggered along the street carrying our huge tin bath.
Freda didn't bother to wonder how I'd be able to make it
the three hundred yards to the washhouse; she'd just load
up the bath and boot me out the door. I knew I would get
into trouble if I dragged the bath, so I had to hold it out in
front of me. It was back-breaking work, and every few
steps I had to stop and put it down.

When I got to the wash house, I'd hand my shilling over and take the yellow ticket the lady behind the counter held out to me. Inside the building, on the ground floor, there were huge sinks with big copper taps along one wall. I'd put my tin bath down next to one of them, thus bagging it for Freda, who would be along later.

Doing the laundry would take Freda a good part of the day. First she'd use the plunger and scrubbing board to wash our clothes and sheets. After each load, she'd use the mangle to wring as much water as she could from them; then she'd dump them in one of the big steel spinners in the middle of the room. Along the side wall were wooden drying racks in heated compartments. Freda would pull one of them out, hang her clothes on it, and leave them drying there until the next load was ready. Lastly, she did some of the ironing, bringing the rest home for me to do.

Upstairs at the wash house were the public baths, and once a month I was allowed to go there. I'd run along our street with my towel, relishing the thought of a long soak. I paid my money and walked up the stairs to where there were several green-painted cubicles. The lady attendant was small and fat, with a big booming voice, and her curls tucked away in a hairnet.

Once in my cubicle, it was quite a task for me to get into the high bath; but, once in, I'd call to the lady attendant to put in the water.

Then came the fun bit: 'More hot, please! . . . That's enough! . . . More cold!'

When the bath was nice and full, and steaming hot, I'd lie back in the water. The tub was so big that I could swim in it. Once or twice I got into trouble for splashing the floor as I used to sit on the end of the bath and then slide down it in a whoosh of water.

I loved bathtime so much that I'd have liked to have stayed there all day, but our time was sharply monitored.

'Time's up, number three!' bawled the small lady with the big voice. And then the fun was over for another month.

Chapter Seven

'Freda, we've got a meeting at the house on Thursday.' My father was sitting in his armchair, newspaper on his knees, relaxing after work.

'You'd better get Judy trained up so that she doesn't let us down. I don't want her misbehaving.'

It was my third week in Wood Street and, although my dad and Freda had been out to a couple of Spiritualist meetings at other people's houses, I had yet to be introduced to the whole pantomime. With his slick-backed hair, trimmed goatee, herringbone-tweed jacket, and shoes as shiny as conkers, my dad certainly looked the part of preacher-showman. And now it was Freda's job to make sure I played my part perfectly too.

'Right, Missy,' said Freda. 'You'll do exactly as I say. If you botch it on Thursday, I'll give you a hiding you'll never forget.'

She told me to go to the top of the stairs. 'I'll want you in your nighty, hair brushed and ready for when I give the word. Right, let's start.'

'Judy, sweetie, it's time for bed now. Come and say goodnight.' I stood at the top of the stairs in amazement. Freda was using a saccharine, smarmy voice I'd never heard before.

Then it was back to her usual rough tone. 'Come on, don't just stand there gawping. Get a move on. Come down.'

I walked down the stairs and followed her to the living-room door. Freda went over and sat on the arm of a chair. 'Now, I want you to say goodnight to our visitors. Go on, say it.'

I mumbled goodnight. My eyes were lowered to the floor as usual. I wasn't used to having to talk, and didn't like it one bit.

'Oh for Christ's sake! Look me in the eyes and say it nicer than that. And for goodness sake, smile!'

I had another go. This time I managed to make a better show of it.

I came back from school on Thursday to find a flowery flannel nightdress lying on my bed. I stayed upstairs in my room and when I heard the first guest arrive, got changed into it, and brushed my hair. At seven-thirty on the dot, I heard Freda's voice, sweet and loving, calling from the bottom of the stairs.

'Judy darling, time for bed, my love,' my pantomime mother trilled. 'Come and say goodnight.'

I walked down the stairs and entered the front room. There were four people sitting around the table on wooden chairs. My father was at the head, looking like he was acting the part of Christ at the Last Supper.

Can't they see this is all fake? I thought to myself as I delivered my lines.

'Night-night . . . night-night.'

Freda handed me a cup of warm milk and kissed me on the cheek. It was all I could do not to flinch or wipe my face where she'd touched it.

One of the ladies sitting at the table was obviously charmed. 'What a lovely daughter you have,' she said to Freda. 'What beautiful manners!'

I'm not her daughter! I thought savagely to myself as I went back upstairs. How I hated having to pretend that I was!

After that evening, I used to go regularly with Dad and Freda to their seances. They wanted me there to help them act the perfect close-knit family —after the Cheshire circle had kicked him out, my father was determined not to botch things up in Hulme. Freda and I were both under his tyrannical scrutiny, and if I so much as creaked my chair whilst the spirit was coming through, or if Freda got a word wrong in her opening prayer, we'd be snarled at in the bus on the way home.

My dad had been brought up to believe he had special gifts. His mother was a staunch Spiritualist and had doted on her youngest son to such an extent that he grew up thinking he really was the Messiah. Dad's initials were J.C.R., and he often used to swagger about it, saying it stood for Jesus Christ Reigns. Occasionally, in an argument with Freda, he'd tower over her, bellowing, 'Do you know *who* you're talking to?' Then I'd see the spittle on his beard and realise he really was mad.

My father was an ambitious man. He wanted to be as famous as Harry Edwards, a well-known spiritualist in the 1950s, and to retire at 35, having made loads of money opening his own sanctuaries. Dad and Freda were always hatching plans, and squirrelled away every spare penny. And they made a fair bit from the gullible ladies who hung on his every word at the seances and healings. When a session was over, my father would never ask for money directly but would winkle it out of his clients with a manipulative phrase like, 'We all help each other. What I do for you, you'll do for me.' And, as the blue-rinsed ladies eagerly lifted their handbags to retrieve their purses, I'd catch Dad casting a sly glance at Freda.

Whilst it was obvious to me that Dad's whole act was a complete fraud, it was strange that he somehow believed his own myth, as, even more oddly, did Freda, who delighted in playing his subservient handmaiden. She loved the whole spiritualist set up and, even though she was often the brunt of my father's mean-spiritedness and towering rages, she was still enthralled by dad's showy charisma. I found it hard to believe Freda could still find him attractive in any way. I'd seen the monstrous bully he was at home and couldn't swallow the sudden switch to loving preacher-man. I simply hated him for it, and cringed when I heard him turn on his fake charm and smarmy, educated voice at the prayer meetings.

'I've got somebody here called George ... anyone know someone who's departed this world called George?' Silence. 'Or a Geoff? ... Yes, we have!'

His sneaky tricks. and the way he'd turn it when he could see he wasn't connecting with his audience, seemed so obvious to me; but the audience loved it, and hung on his every word. I used to watch the lonely old ladies, their mouths hanging open slightly as he performed, and detest my father for preying on their weakness.

The first time I went with Dad and Freda to a psychic healing, I witnessed the most extraordinary piece of theatre. This time it was a one-to-one session at the house of an old lady who was in agony with an ulcer on her leg. Barely able to leave her chair, she was lonely and in pain – the perfect prey for my father to pounce on.

'Come in, come in Mr Richardson,' Mrs Hardy said, hobbling back to her chair. I looked at her swollen purple ankle below the bandages. 'Hello, lovey,' she said kindly to me, and I was ashamed when I realized she'd seen me staring at her leg.

When my father went into a trance, he shuddered a little and his eyes seemed to be looking at a far distant place. His voice changed completely as he came under the control of the 'spirit guide'. In time, I came to recognize all of the spirits that came through my father, each one from a different realm of the spirit world. This time, Mrs Hardy got 'Dr X', the lowest of the spirits.

As Dad took on the persona of Dr X, who, he explained later to Mrs Hardy, was a surgeon from Matabeleland, he started speaking in a very posh voice. Even his gestures changed. He hunkered down in his chair (Dr X being a smaller man than my father) and began to mime the act of cleansing his mouth of tobacco bits, his tongue delicately slipping between his teeth as he removed imaginary strands between thumb and forefinger. Then he got down to work in earnest.

Mrs Hardy watched the psychic surgeon perform his miraculous operation with intense belief. And my dad did put on an amazing show. He moved his hands around her leg as if he really was working with a scalpel. Every now and then, he'd pause to take another instrument from the invisible hand of his psychic nurse.

'Now, you may feel a twinge in your leg as I move my hands over it,' my father said in his most educated voice. 'Ah, there's the scab now. I just need to clean the wound. Now you'll feel my hand passing warmth through your body. This is spirit healing you.'

At that, he took some deep breaths and started to sigh

loudly, drawing the air in through his nose and out of his mouth. His hands were shaking and his eyelids fluttered.

Mrs Hardy was tearful with gratitude at the end of the session. 'Mr Richardson, my leg feels almost right again. You really are a miracle worker!' And she really did look better when she got up to pay my father and show us to the door, and wasn't limping half as badly.

As the months went on, I became more familiar with Dr X. He was in the lowest world of the seven heavenly realms and so, being more earthly, came through most often. My father instructed me to call him Uncle Toby. The big shot from the number one realm, Chief Running Water, hardly ever came through. When he did, my father acted as though it was a supremely magical moment which we were all blessed to have witnessed. Other guides were Pedro, a Mexican bandit, who'd been shot; Imaki the Eskimo (he was very nosy); and Dr Samakasan, a highly educated Hindu man. Chief Running Water and Pedro both sounded like something out of a Western. I thought their accents were very over the top, especially when my father overdid it with his 'Adios amigo'; but it made for a good show.

One evening, we visited the house of the brother of Freda's friend Madge. We were ushered into the parlour where a few guests had already gathered. This was a key moment for my dad, and I watched him ease himself around the room gleaning as much information from the guests about their loves and losses, money troubles, and future plans as he possibly could. They seemed so eager to unload their stories.

I stood apart from the guests, feeling self-conscious in my frilled party dress, hair pulled back from my face with a Kirby grip. I found it hard to take my eyes off my father, partly through habitual fear, but also because he was the kind of man people did tend look at. Now, as I watched his elegant six-foot frame bending caringly over a dark-haired young woman, I thought he could have been Gregory Peck. He was acting the priestly role so well. I could tell from the woman's haunted-looking eyes, and the quiet way she was talking to him, that she'd lost someone dear to her and was telling my dad about it. He'd scented her grief and longing a mile off, and I knew he'd move in on her later once the seance was in full swing.

When everyone had gathered at last, we were taken by our hosts into the living room, where there was a large table, big enough to seat the twelve people present. I was told to sit on a stool at the other end of the room. I knew I couldn't move a muscle, as the slightest creak might earn me a beating later. It was perishing at my end of the room, and my dress wasn't at all warm, being made of sober blue cotton with a frill around the bottom and having a high-necked white bodice. All very demure and proper. Just the ticket for the daughter of a minister.

By now the group were all seated at the table, my father at the head, and Freda the dutiful at his right hand. The session began with my father's introduction, delivered in the rich tones he saved for these occasions. He could have been a bishop.

'We are gathered here this evening ...' he intoned, and the faces of his little flock were instantly glued to his. *Let the show begin.*

After my Dad's address, the group recited the seven principles of Spiritualism. '*The fatherhood of God; the brotherhood of man; communion of spirits and the ministry of angels; the continuous existence of the human soul; personal responsibility; compensation and retribution hereafter for all good and evil deeds done on earth; eternal progress open to every soul.'* They had the fingers of both hands linked in a special grip, not in the way you'd usually pray.

After the recitation of the seven principles came Freda's opening prayer. While she spoke, my father slowly began to change as the spirit entered his body. As he pretended to go into a trance, he squashed himself down in his chair and started snorting through his nose. His hands were on his thighs, palms up, eyes half closed. Then his head lolled backwards.

'Good evening everyone, I'm Imaki. Thank you all for coming.' I could sense a shiver of pleasure run through the circle of people as they heard the eskimo's squeaky little voice. They were usually given Dr X, and I knew that Imaki was a rare treat for them. My dad must have judged that they were due for a change, or perhaps he thought that someone in the group that evening might give him a bigger donation than usual. The only time we ever got Chief Running Water was at the Rippons, a rich couple who lived in a large Victorian villa at the posh end of town. They were the most prized members of my dad's circle, and he always made sure they were kept happy.

Now it was time for Imaki's message for the day. At this point, my father started talking in riddles and parables.

'The end of the world is coming, my friends, and the sound will be like rain falling on a hot tin roof.' I thought this sounded pretty ridiculous, particularly as it was delivered in Imaki's high-pitched voice; but the assembled company wagged their heads and whispered, 'Thank you, Imaki.'

There was a pause, and everyone sat still, waiting. Then my father started speaking again.

'I can see somebody ... a man ... an old man. He has a message for you.' He was staring now at a plump woman sitting opposite. 'He had a problem, here.' My father cupped his hands over his chest, a favourite ruse for it could mean heart, lungs, or quite a lot of other things.

'That's my dad, George,' the woman said. 'Died last year. It was his second heart attack.'

'George has a message for you,' my father said. 'What's that? What's that?' He cupped his hand to his ear, acting as if George wasn't delivering it clearly enough. Then a pause. 'You are going to move to a new place and that's the right thing to do.'

'Amazing. That's right!' the woman announced, eyes sparkling. 'We're thinking of moving house.'

'I can see the sea, and smell salt in the air,' said my father, elaborating on his theme. (He'd already heard that she was thinking of moving house to Southport.)

'Oh, that's right; we're planning to retire to the seaside,' she said, 'I'm glad that George approves.'

My father moved on from one person to the next, making sure that each had a little something to go home with: messages from aunties, grannies, sons lost in the war, dogs and cats. At times, he interrupted the proceedings with a little piece of extra theatre, allowing the nosy character of his Eskimo spirit guide full rein.

'What have you got over there? What's that? What's behind there?' His darting eyes looked around the room impishly. It occurred to me that if Imaki really was an all-knowing spirit, then he wouldn't have to ask.

Dad's eyes were now fixed on the settee and he acted as if he could see something there. Then they moved to the dark-haired young woman I'd seen him talking to earlier.

'I can see two little children. They're playing behind the settee and keep peeping out.'

At my father's words the woman broke down. 'My babies! My little ones!' she whispered in a sob. 'I lost them at five months.'

'Well, they've come to tell you they're happy now. They're in Summerland,' said my father. (Summerland was where children's spirits went to when they died.) 'They want you to know they're safe and that their nurses are looking after them very well.'

'Thank you! Oh, thank you! My babies ...' At this, the woman's voice faded to nothing and she put her hand over her eyes for a few moments.

I sat there on my stool, disgusted. I felt almost dirty listening to my dad, knowing what a con it all was.

After the readings were finished, the group were handed tea in china cups and corned-beef sandwiches. There was a happy glow in the room, and the chatter was now very relaxed. Behind the kitchen door our host was quietly collecting envelopes of money from the guests; as my father and Freda said their goodbyes, the collection was pressed into Dad's hand with a murmured, 'For your sanctuary.'

Chapter Eight

My father didn't allow me to make any friends in our neighbourhood, and I was desperately lonely. I'd spend hours whispering into my teddy bear's ear, pretending she was my best friend. Dad didn't want Mum knowing where we were and he'd had enough of people poking their nose in his business, so I was told to keep my trap shut at all times. He didn't want it getting out that Freda and he weren't married, or that she wasn't my mother.

The other reason he didn't want me mixing with anyone was pure snobbery. Dad lorded it over the others in Wood Street and, as we had the end of terrace house, bigger than the rest and with a yard of its own, he could look down on everybody else.

Dad didn't let me go to the same school as the other kids in our street. Instead I had to walk quite a way, across three main roads, to Duke Street Primary, where the other children all knew each other. They'd played together after school since they were little and already had their gangs. I was just an outsider.

Sometimes, after I'd finished my chores in the evening, I'd stand on the dustbin in our yard and look over the wall at the kids playing in the alley. I'd watch them playing

Jerries and Tommies, brandishing pieces of wood, and making the sound of rattling bullets – 'ta-ta-ta-ta' – their voices ringing out in the alley. I longed with all my heart to join in.

The Wood Street kids thought I was odd for not playing out in the street. They thought I didn't go to Lloyd Street School with them because I was a snob, and it only made things worse that I wasn't allowed to talk to them. When they taunted me on the way to school, I just gritted my teeth and walked on. I really wanted to go over and ask if I could play with them later, but was too scared my dad might find out.

I used to stand against the railings of the enormous playground of Duke Street School every breaktime, watching the other kids. The girls would be playing skipping or clapping games or sitting hunched over their marbles, cross-legged in a circle. Many of the boys would be playing a game with their cigarette cards, a bit like bowls except they flicked the cards. Others would be playing tiddlywinks with bottle tops. After weeks of standing and watching, longing with all my heart to join in, I thought of a plan.

The next morning, after doing my chores, I carefully opened the sock drawer in the living room and took out Freda's purse, which she kept hidden there. I took sixpence from it. I didn't stop to reflect that what I'd done was wrong, my desire to find a friend was so great. I had a grand plan which was driving me forward and nothing would get in my way.

On the way to school, I stopped at Allens, the corner shop, and bought a large bag of sweets – mint imperials, toffees, bullseyes, and gobstoppers – and put them in my pocket. At breaktime, I went into the playground as usual but, instead of standing by the railings on my own, I walked over to a group of girls who were playing marbles.

'Hey, anyone want a sweet?' I tried hard to look as though it didn't matter much to me either way. Inside, though, I felt as if all my future happiness depended on how these girls reacted. At first it seemed as if my plan to find some friends had worked as they all gathered around me. But the attention didn't last long, and when the bag was empty the girls returned to their game and I was left standing outside their enchanted circle, unsure of what to do. Then I felt even lonelier than ever.

In my mind there was only one thing to do, and that was to buy more sweets. I wanted to feel that warm glow again, to have the girls huddle around me again and say nice things.

The next morning I stole another sixpence from Freda's purse. She hadn't noticed the missing money the day before, or perhaps she'd thought my dad had taken it. In the playground that day, I approached a different group of girls, who were playing a ball game. Two girls each had a ball and the others were watching intently while they threw it one to the other. I knew the song off by heart:

> Solomon Grundy,
> Born on a Monday,
> Christened on Tuesday,
> Married on Wednesday,
> Took ill on Thursday,
> Worse on Friday,
> Died on Saturday,
> Buried on Sunday,
> This is the end of Solomon Grundy.

One of the girls dropped her ball at that moment and before another girl could take her place, I stepped forward.

'Anyone want a toffee? I've got loads.' I held out the bag with the confident smile I'd been practising with Susie at home.

Again it happened. The girls gathered round, drenched me with cupboard love for five minutes, then went back to their game.

The next day it was the same story; but on the evening of the fourth day, when I got back from school, Freda was waiting for me. As soon as I saw her face I knew what was coming. My first instinct was to run but I stood rooted to the spot, unable to breathe or speak. Freda looked more livid than I'd ever seen her, her face white as chalk and below it a nasty red rash staining her neck.

'Mrs Allen told me what you've been up to, you little thief!' Freda was holding her purse in her hand. 'If you want it so much, you can take the bloody lot!' At that, she took a handful of change out of it and threw it in my face.

Almost panting with rage, Freda grabbed a wooden coat hanger from the table and came at me. With one hand she held the collar of my coat to stop me getting away; with the other she beat me around the head with the hanger. The force of her blows almost knocked my teeth into the back of my head and I tasted blood. The pain of it was shattering and I desperately tried to protect my head with my arm.

Later on, as I lay on my bed upstairs hugging Susie to my chest, my whole body was throbbing with pain and shock. I felt along the edge of my teeth with my tongue, and it was then that I realized that two of my teeth were broken.

Freda must have decided that a beating wasn't enough punishment for me. So the next day she came to my school and told the headmaster what I'd done.

If I'd had trouble making friends before, now Freda made it quite impossible. At assembly the next day, the headmaster called for hush in the hall before he spoke:

'I've had a visit from a most distressed mother yesterday and I was very disturbed at what she told me.' At this, twenty rows of expectant faces all swivelled about, looking to see who the guilty child might be, half revelling in the drama, and half worrying it might be them.

'Judith Richardson? Where is she?' The headmaster scanned our row. 'Will you please stand up?'

The blood was thundering in my ears and I didn't immediately get to my feet. My form teacher then caught my eye and motioned with her hand for me to get up. I felt a hundred pairs of eyes fixed on me as I stood there, dreading what the headmaster was going to say next.

'You repeatedly stole money from your mother's purse so you could buy sweets,' He paused and a ripple went through the children in the hall. 'I'm sure we all agree', he went on, 'that it was a shocking thing that Judith did – deceiving her mother in this way.'

The headmaster was in his stride now and took us through the Ten Commandments, told a parable about a thief, and generally drummed it in that I was a wicked sinner and not the sort of child he wanted in his school.

I was aching to tell them, *I bought the sweets for the others. I never ate a single one. I only wanted a friend.*

From that moment on, the teachers and pupils at Duke Street never let me forget that I was a thief. It was as if an indelible brand had been burned into my forehead. Weeks later, when my form teacher asked for volunteers to collect the dinner money, I was careful not to raise my hand but she picked on me all the same, saying, 'I'm glad that you didn't offer, Judith. We certainly wouldn't be able to trust you with money after what you did, would we children?'

Strangely enough, the first friend I had in Wood Street came via my father – the very person who'd made sure I was always friendless. Dad came home after work one day, a couple of months after I'd been sent to Hulme, and peeping out of his pocket was a little puppy that one of his workmates had given him. He called her Gyp.

Gyp became the friend I'd been yearning for. Each morning, when I got up at first light, she would be waiting for me downstairs, wagging her tail in welcome. Suddenly, my chores didn't seem half as miserable with this alert little pup at my side. She was remarkably patient with me when I wanted to play doctors and nurses, and even let me dress her up in my clothes. She quickly took over from Susie as my number one confidante, and when I got back from school, and had finished my afternoon chores, I'd lie on my bed telling her about my day. She'd sit with her paw on my knee and watch me with bright, intelligent eyes.

Once, when my dad lifted his arm to hit me, Gyp jumped up and grabbed his sleeve, growling menacingly at him. She was a brave little dog and the best thing that had ever happened to me.

It was through Gyp that I met Edna Hillyard. The dogs in our neighbourhood were all allowed to roam the streets during the day. No one bothered about collars or leads. When I left for school, Gyp stayed in Wood Street, playing with other dogs and scavenging for scraps. I used to wish I could hang around with her instead of having to go to school.

I used to dash home in the afternoons, desperate to play with Gyp. When she ran up to greet me I'd squat down and put my arms around her neck and she'd lick my face. It was on one of these afternoons that I met Edna.

Edna lived two doors up from us, the youngest child in a large, ramshackle family. On the day we first spoke to each other, she was sitting on the step with her dog eating a hunk of bread. I walked over to Gyp, who was sniffing around Edna's large, friendly-looking mutt. The dog looked twice the weight of the girl, who was an under-nourished scrap of a thing with thin, pale hair. She had a sharp little elfin face and must have been a year or two younger than me.

'What's your name?'

Edna eyed me with bright eyes, like an inquisitive little robin. I didn't answer her at first, too nervous to open my mouth. My back felt all prickly – I was sure that a hundred eyes were watching me. In my imaginings, Freda's spies were always everywhere.

'Judy.' I barely moved my lips.

'Mine's Edna,' the girl said. 'Why can't you play out?'

'Not allowed.'

'Why not?' Edna wasn't giving up.

'Dunno.' Part of me was wanting to continue with our conversation – what there was of it – but I simply didn't dare. And so I called Gyp and went home.

A few days later, I was walking down the alley next to our house with Gyp when I saw Edna standing on her own, scuffing the ground with a tatty plimsol. She looked bored. Gyp ran over to her dog and began to sniff his bottom.

'Bonzo and Gyp are best friends,' Edna said. 'Do you want to come and play?'

'Someone'll see us.'

'Not if we go to Lloyd Street.' Edna said. 'Come on.'

I followed her and once we were a few streets away, in the road that skirted her school, I finally relaxed.

'Can you do handstands?' Edna asked, immediately flipping upside down. Her arms looked as though they'd be too spindly to carry her weight and she didn't do a great job of it. I was ace at handstands – naturally bendy and totally fearless. If you've been bashed and beaten all your life I guess you don't feel fear like other kids.

Edna gave up doing handstands and watched me for a bit, looking impressed. Then she walked along the low wall that skirted the pavement, her arms stretched out on either side to help her balance.

'Can you play hopscotch?' I asked Edna.

'Course!'

'Come on, let's look for a bit of slate.' In those days, you could always find broken roof slates amongst the general rubble of our streets and alleys. Kids didn't dare nick the teachers' chalk, so slate was all they had to mark out the hopscotch grid.

We found some bits of slate and I drew the numbers and squares on the ground. We then spent a happy half hour, throwing the piece of slate and hopping and jumping from one square to the next. I don't know if Edna sensed how momentous this was for me. She wouldn't have known that I'd always had to play on my own.

Edna and I played together a lot after that and she quickly became a huge part of my life. Every morning, on waking, Edna was the first thing I thought about, and she was the last thing in my mind before going to sleep. I used to get my afternoon chores done in double-quick time so that I could go and play hopscotch with her.

Edna and I talked a lot too. I wasn't used to talking like a child about a child's things, and it was exhilarating. I loved to hear about her school and what she'd been doing that day. Later, in my room, I'd weave fantasies around Lord Street School. It became a sort of Mallory Towers in my mind, a place of high jinks and undying friendships.

With ten mouths to feed, there wasn't much to go around at Edna's. Despite their problems, however, Edna's mother was always welcoming. Mrs Hillyard was a big bruiser of a woman with raggedy hair and very large arms. The first time that Edna took me into her house I was shocked that things were so basic. In the Hillyards' front room there was just one big table, covered with newspaper instead of a cloth. Other than a bench, there was no other furniture in the room at all. I think Mr Hillyard spent too much of his wages at the pub. Lying in bed at night, I used to hear him singing the Johnnie Ray song 'Just Walking in the Rain', on his way home after closing time. Once, in the yellow light of the gas lamp, I watched him from my window. He was weaving his way up the street in the smoggy air, a bleary-faced wafer of a man. I felt there was something a little bit tragic about him.

Edna was always hungry. When I saw her sitting on the step with the hunk of bread she'd been given for her tea I worried that her bare knees looked terribly bony and bluish. Once, when we went into Mrs Allen's corner shop, I saw Edna nick two Walls sausages from the window and stuff them under her jumper. As soon as we got outside, she hungrily crammed them raw into her mouth.

I quickly became obsessed with finding warm food for Edna. All I needed to do was to come up with a plan to get hold of some. I decided that I wanted to buy her a bag of chips from the chippy at the end of the road. The hard thing was working out how. There was no way I'd be venturing near Freda's purse again.

I knew that if you took enough newspapers to the fish and chip shop they'd give you a bag of chips, because they needed the papers to wrap the food in. I soon came up with a plan to get a stack. There were two papers that gave the results of all the football matches, the football pinks and the football greens. The pinks were delivered at four or five every Saturday afternoon.

I walked along the streets in the wake of the paperboy, nicking the papers from the doorsteps. At the fish and chip shop, the lady behind the counter didn't seem to notice or care that I was handing her a stack of brand-new football pinks. She gave me a big bag of chips and some scraps – the batter bits – for free. I couldn't wait to give them to Edna. I would have run down the street but was nervous of dropping the bag.

'Mrs Hillyard, is Edna in?' I stood on the step, holding the bag of chips behind my back

'Edna!' Mrs Hillyard shouted up the stairs. 'Judy's here to see you.'

Edna ran down the stairs, two at a time, and came outside, closing the door behind her.

I held out the bag of chips and scraps.

'Cor, how did you get those?' Edna's eyes were on stalks.

'I nicked the football pinks, but don't tell anyone,' I replied. 'They're for you. I'm full already.'

I watched with enormous satisfaction as Edna sat on the step and got stuck into the chips. When she'd finished she showed me her tummy. I'd seen a picture in a book at school of a snake that had just eaten a frog and it looked just like that.

Edna didn't need to say thank you. Just seeing her eat was enough for me. But it was lovely when she gave me a big, gap-toothed grin all the same.

The next Saturday morning, I was sitting on the step with Edna laughing at Gyp and Bonzo chasing each others' heels and barking. Dad and Freda were both out and I knew they wouldn't be back until later. Edna had been waiting for the past hour or more for her brother, Bill, to arrive. She wanted to be the first to greet him, so we were posted there as look-outs.

'Me mam says I've got to go into hospital,' Edna said.

'What's wrong with you?' I asked, remembering my weeks spent tied to the bars of the cot at Hope Hospital.

'Got something wrong with my tummy,' she said cheer-fully. 'Do you get jelly and custard in hospital?'

'Yeah. Every day,' I said reassuringly, knowing that food was top of the agenda for Edna. 'When are you going?'

'Dunno. Next week, I think.'

We sat for a moment in silence. Then Bonzo tore himself away from Gyp and ran off down the street barking, his tail waving madly. Edna jumped up.

'Bill!' she cried. 'It's him. He's here!' Edna tore off after Bonzo and I followed at a more hesitant pace, feeling a bit shy. Edna had told me all about her glamourous brother Bill, who was a soldier in the army.

Bill didn't disappoint. He was dressed in his khakis and cap and had an almost American swagger, with clean-cut looks to match. He was obviously delighted to see Edna and scooped her up, swinging her round in a circle.

'Hello there, littl'un!' Bill put her down and turned to me. 'Who's your friend?'

'This is Judy,' Edna said. 'She lives in the house at the end.'

'Well, you can share this with Judy, then,' Bill said, holding out a banana. We'd never seen a banana before. Edna held it tentatively, having no idea what to do with it.

'How do you eat it?' she asked Bill.

'Here, like this,' he said, laughing, and peeled back the skin in strips. 'Go on, have a bite.'

Edna and I then took a little bite each. I thought the banana tasted horrid and felt slimy. Since my two rice pudding episodes I never could eat anything slimy.

'Ugh!' said Edna, handing the banana back to Bill, who polished it off.

'Better go see the old ma and pa,' Bill then said. 'Come on, Eddie. Nice meeting you, Judy.'

I went back to our house then and lay a while on my bed. I added Bill to my list of fantasy heroes and made up a Tommies and Jerries adventure, with Bill in the starring role.

I didn't see Edna again before she went to hospital, and life felt pretty flat when she'd gone. I'd got used to seeing her most days. I kept thinking of her on her own in a ward with no one to play with and wondered what I could do to show I was thinking of her. I decided to give her one of my books, not a library book, but one I'd been given by one of my dad's Spiritualist circle. The book was one of my favourites, *What Katy Did*, and I reckoned that Edna would love it too. It seemed an especially appropriate story. Katy gets crippled after a fall and can't run around with her friends like before. Now Edna was stuck in hospital she might like to imagine she was Katy.

I took the book round to Mrs Hillyard and asked her to give it to Edna the next time she went to the hospital.

Edna's mum looked kindly at me. I'd come to realize over the past few weeks that this big-boned, dour woman had a very warm heart.

'That's kind of you, Judy,' she said, smiling. I only realized then where Edna got her gap-toothed grin, as I'd never seen her Mum smiling before. I suppose it was a tough life looking after ten kids with hardly two pennies to rub together.

'How long before she comes out, Mrs Hillyard?' I asked.

'Oh, a little while yet, probably another couple of weeks,' she told me. 'But she'll be tickled you lent her the book, she really will.'

I think that becoming fond of Edna had made me open out, like a moth from its cocoon, in the weeks I'd got to know her. I was happier and more relaxed. I was also less on my guard.

Evelyn, one of Edna's sisters, knocked at our door a few days later. When Freda opened it, she was instantly tense, her mouth set in a hard line.

'Yes? What are you doing here?'

'Me mam asked me to bring this back to Judy,' Evelyn said. 'She said to be sure and tell her that Edna really liked it.'

Freda, eyes sparking with fury, snatched the book from Evelyn and slammed the door in her face.

'Judy!'

I knew it was bad from her tone. I had the crazy idea of jumping from my window to escape but went downstairs instead. Before I could reach the bottom of the stairs, Freda made a lunge at me and grabbed my arm. She whacked me across the face with the book then kicked me hard in the shins so that my legs buckled under me.

'I'm going to burn them all, every bloody book of yours!' she screamed at me. 'You lying little runt. You're never, ever having anything to do with that disgusting, filthy family again, you hear that?'

Freda made me go round then and there to tell Mrs Hillyard that I wasn't allowed to play with Edna any more. I felt ashamed and desperate as I stood on the doorstep delivering the message. Edna's mum wasn't angry – in fact, she looked sorry for me – but I sensed that she was furious at Freda for being a stuck-up cow, thinking her daughter was too good to mix with their family.

Mrs Hillyard saw my face had a welt across it from where the book had cut into it. 'Are you alright, lovey?' she asked me. But I couldn't answer her and ran back home, where there was much more trouble to come.

By the time I got back, Freda had taken all my books and locked them away – she must have had second thoughts about burning them. She carried on raging about the Hillyards, calling them every name under the sun; and of course when my dad got home from work she told him what I'd done. She usually refrained from telling him anything that would make him go off the deep end, but this time she must have thought she'd get found out if she didn't.

My dad was madder than I'd ever seen him before. The idea that I had been talking to people on our street frightened him and that they might have found out that Freda wasn't his wife and that I wasn't her daughter sent him right over the edge. Everything he'd built in Hulme, the whole idyllic family picture, was in peril because of me. He must have thought the whole house of cards was about to fall down around him. The fact that I'd been mixing with the Hillyards, a family he considered far beneath him, only made it worse.

My father rose slowly from his chair to stand over me. He let out great snorting breaths from his nose and the veins stood out in his neck. 'How dare you betray me?' he hissed. For a moment I was icy calm, like being in the eye of the storm. I could see flecks of spittle in his goatee.

He really laid into me then, bouncing me all over the place; kicking, punching, throwing me across the room. Starting in the living room, then through the kitchen, right up the stairs and into my bedroom. I knew that he wanted to beat me so he could see me cry, and because I wouldn't cry he beat me even more.

All the while my father was punching and kicking me, there was a thought, a whisper, inside my head. *You can beat the outside of me all you like but you're not going to get the inside of me. You're not going to see me cry.*

Each time my father threw me across the bedroom floor, he'd pull me up by the arm and kick me across the room again. Freda must have realized that if he went on like that, he'd kill me and I heard her crying, 'Stop it, Jack. Stop it, Jack. Stop it, Jack.'

When Dad had finished with me, Freda helped me down to the living room where she sat me on her knee and asked if I wanted anything to eat. She must have been really worried. My father was sitting in the chair opposite, staring into space and breathing fast. Sitting on Freda's knee, touching her, made me panic even more and as soon as I could, I got off and struggled back upstairs to my room.

When I was lying on my bed that night, I had the feeling that I wasn't actually there. I was somewhere else, though I didn't know where it was; I couldn't picture the place. I must have slept then because the next thing I remember it was the middle of the night. There was a frantic hammering in my head and my throat was parched. My eyes were burning like hot coals and all my senses, my skin, my eyes, were palpitating. It was terrifying as I had no control at all – it wasn't like when you have a sore place which can be eased by rubbing it: my whole body was pulsating. It was as if it had a life of its own. Rebelling. The pulses in my eyes were pumping, pumping, pumping. I couldn't see anything; I was totally blind. The pulses were so strong that I thought my eyes were going to pop out of my head.

When I woke in the morning, my head felt as if it was twice its size. I dragged myself downstairs somehow; nothing would have stopped me doing my chores. Something bigger than the pain in my body drove me forward. I think I knew that if I didn't carry on I'd collapse. It wasn't courage; it was simply that I was scared to death.

I couldn't pick up the buckets of coal because the muscles in my arms had been torn and stretched by my father dragging and flinging me. I found the strength from somewhere, though, and pulled the buckets, inch by painful inch, across the yard and into the kitchen.

That night, as I stood by my bedroom window, I was filled with an intense desire to escape. I'd felt it before, but now it was burning so strong. I gazed at the gas lamp and wondered if I'd be able to catch the cross bars on the post if I jumped from the window sill. I'd seen the boys in the alley playing at cowboys and lassoing the bars on the gas lamp with a piece of rope. They'd make a loop seat, sit on it, and swing round and round the post. If I had that rope now, I thought, I could throw a loop myself and swing down on it. I'd read so many Enid Blyton stories, full of daring escapes with knotted sheets, that I yearned to do the same. Nobody would see me, nobody would know where I'd gone.

Then the fear took hold of me again. *But where would I go? How would I find my mother? Where would I start? Where was Patricroft? Where did they live? How do I get there?* The questions piled on top of me until I felt suffocated. In the end I got to thinking, *What if I get found? What would he do to me if I was brought back?*

And then I felt crushed by it all. Even looking at the stars, which I'd always imagined were my real family, loving me from a distance, didn't make me feel any better.

Chapter Nine

I never played with Edna again after that. Life went on in Wood Street, but it wasn't the same. Sometimes I looked at one of the gaps in our row where a house had been bombed and felt like there was a huge gaping hole just like that inside me. I was still here, going on the same as before, but it was different now.

Things got much better when I moved up to Miss Williams' class at Sunday School. I was eight years old by this time and had been going to Sunday School at Bridgewater Hall every week since I'd arrived at Hulme. It suited my dad and Freda to let me go as they were out all day Sundays at the Spiritualist church.

I liked Sunday School. Because the hall was a little distance away from where we lived the kids didn't know me there, and so they were perfectly friendly, allowing me to join in the activities. We used to sing children's hymns, such as 'Jesus wants me for a pilgrim', and we were taught all about the Scriptures, drawing pictures and making cards. We acted out little bible-story plays, and I soon found that I loved performing.

Miss Williams saw something special in me. She was a tiny person, with big round glasses, like bottle ends, which she never seemed to look through but always over the top of. Her hair was like a close-fitting cap of tiny, tight curls and she'd wear a little blue pillbox hat on top of them on her way to church which matched her suit. Her white blouse was always buttoned right up to her neck.

Soon after Miss Williams had taken over our class, she called me over at the end of the morning.

'Judith, I was wondering if you'd like to join the choir,' she said. 'I don't know if your parents will mind as it will mean your having to attend morning, afternoon and evening services.'

'Nobody's there in the day, Miss, so it wouldn't matter,' I told her.

'Excellent! That settles it then,' she said with a smile. 'We'll start next Sunday.'

The next week, when all the other kids went home with their parents after the morning service, Miss Williams, knowing I had nowhere to go between services, asked me if I'd like to come home with her. She didn't have a family of her own and I reckoned she was probably lonely too. At school, the teachers never seemed to see or care that I was an unhappy child, but I know Miss Williams sensed it immediately, although she never said anything.

Miss Williams lived in an ordinary terraced house like ours, not far from Bridgewater Hall. When we got there, she led the way inside, hanging up her coat and hat on a peg by the door. I did the same. My coat was a cast-off from one of the richer members of my dad's Spiritualist circle and it was much too small for me. I couldn't really lift my arms but I was proud of it all the same. It was red with a hood, just like one Princess Anne had been photographed wearing.

When I walked into the front room, I stopped dead in surprise. It was so cluttered with things that I didn't know quite where to walk. Against one wall there was an organ and facing that a piano. There was sheet music everywhere, on music stands and in piles on a table in the middle of the room. The walls were hung with religious paintings and wooden crosses.

During the week, Miss Williams was a music teacher. Although her Sundays should have been a time of rest, she didn't waste any time but got straight to work with me.

'Now Judith, sit yourself here, dear,' she said pulling out the piano stool. 'I'm going to show you how to hold your hands. That's it, bend your fingers like that. Lift your wrists a little.'

I tried a scale and then, having introduced me to the notes, Miss Williams said she wanted to show me a game that would make them easier to remember.

'I'm going to hide these cards all over the room,' she said with a twinkle. 'And you're going to play the notes in whatever order you find them.'

Miss Williams had a stack of large cards and on each was drawn a musical note and its name. 'Now, hide your eyes, Judith!' she said.

It was much easier to remember the notes after playing the game. When I had collected all the cards, I found it funny when the sounds I made on the piano made no musical sense at all, jumbled as they were. Soon I was trying to swap the order of the cards I'd found so that they made a better tune.

'That's it! Look how quickly you've learned the notes,' said Miss Williams, clapping her hands. 'Well done, Judith. You almost made a scale there.'

Later we practised my singing. Miss Williams was very exacting. I had to stand just right and learn to control my breathing, taking in the air from somewhere just above my tummy.

'No ...no ... no ... no ... no,' she intoned if I wavered or went sharp. Then, 'Hooold, hold it!'

When I got it right she clapped her hands and said, 'Clever girl, clever girl!'

After our lessons, Miss Williams brought out a delicate china tea-set and a plate of lovely little iced cakes. They must have cost her a lot of money and I don't imagine she had such fine things every day. It gave me a warm feeling to think she must have bought them just for me.

Chapter Ten

It was a relief when spring brought the warm weather with it. By now my red coat was so small that I'd started walking in a funny way, so I was happy to put it by. I was relieved to be rid of my socks too. I'd been forced by Freda to wear an old pair of my father's, darned at the toes and heels. They were so big for me that the heel came half way up my leg. I used to try and tuck the toe end underneath my foot, but that made it hard to walk.

I never had any new clothes. Freda would bring me the odd thing from piles of clothing people had put by for the jumble and so, except for those evenings when we were doing our perfect family act, I always looked pretty ragged. Because Freda wouldn't dream of spending a penny on me, as well as Dad's old socks I had to wear her cast-off knickers. It was humiliating going to school with her knicker legs flapping around under my skirt. One afternoon, in desperation, I sat down at Freda's sewing machine and had a go at sewing a pleat in the leg material. Luckily no one at school ever saw my huge grey knickers as I used to slip a pair of blue school pants over them before changing into my gym slip. Dad's socks I couldn't hide away.

I was eight years old that May of 1953. I never quite knew what day my birthday was as the occasion was never mentioned, let alone celebrated. It was only years later, when I stole my birth certificate from my father's things, that I found out for certain. I remember then, as I studied the certificate, being desperately disappointed to find that Dad really was my real father, and that I wasn't adopted or stolen as I'd often dreamed I must be. I always longed to be somebody else's kid.

That May, Freda told me we were going to the Isle of Man for a week. My dad had been invited to preach at a Spiritualist gathering there and our ferry fares and bed and breakfast expenses had been paid for. He was hoping that there might be some rich pickings to be made from this new circle.

Although I knew we'd be staying at the seaside, I wasn't at all excited to be going. Somehow I found that leaving behind the routine of my chores caused me more anxiety than having to do them perfectly. Being torn from the safety of my bedroom and books was hard, but leaving Gyp behind was the worst thing of all. I didn't trust Madge to make sure she was fed and her water dish filled and the thought that she might think we weren't ever coming back nagged away at me.

When we reached the Isle of Man, I wasn't allowed to attend any of the seances or gatherings. The first couple of days I hung around the garden of the bed and breakfast or wandered about the streets. On the third day, though, Freda and my dad took me to the beach.

Dad led the way down the steps and onto the sand. The sea was quite far out and there was a huge stretch of beach. It was already busy with families arriving and setting up their stripy windbreaks and deckchairs.

'Stay there and don't move,' my father ordered. I sat down on the sand next to the ice-cream shop. Without glancing my way again, he walked quickly away to join Freda who was waiting up on the promenade.

It was like my first day in the yard at Patricroft again, being told not to move and not knowing how long I'd have to sit there. Only this time there was plenty to watch, and instead of being cold I was warm.

The hours passed to lunchtime, and as the sun rose in the sky I soon became hot and thirsty. Freda hadn't thought to leave me with anything to drink so I had nothing with which to quench my thirst. And, as I watched the picnic baskets being unpacked, my stomach started rumbling too.

I tried to take my mind off my dry mouth and empty tummy by making an ice-cream shop of my own, filling cone-shaped shells with sand and pretending to ask customers what flavour they wanted. I piled up tiny shells and stones and used them as money.

I didn't dare walk down to the water's edge to have a paddle, much as I would have liked to. I was too fearful that my dad might come back at that moment and find I wasn't in the place he'd left me. It wasn't just his wrath I was afraid of – I was scared that I might be left on the beach forever, like a towel someone had forgotten to take home with them at the end of the day. If I wasn't there, exactly where he'd told me to wait, would he bother to look for me at all?

I watched two little boys covering their dad with sand. He lay there patiently, even when they sprinkled it on his face and made him snort. I kept thinking he was going to jump up with a bellow of rage, but when he did move at last, he rose slowly, pretending to be a sea monster from the deep, and grabbed his little boys by the ankle. Their screams soon turned to giggles. I couldn't imagine anyone daring to bury my father with sand.

The sun was dipping in the sky now and the deckchairs were throwing huge shadows across the sand. Most of the families had left and the last stragglers were gathering up their belongings, their sunburned skin looking a darker pink than before. Even as the last family walked past me to go up the stone steps, no one paused to wonder what I was doing there all alone. Not until the deckchair man came up to me.

He was a middle-aged man in vest and shorts and I watched him as he folded and stacked the chairs. By now, he was the only other person on the beach. Just him and me.

It was only when he'd finished his job and had turned to leave that he saw me. He hesitated for a moment, standing there staring at me; then he came over.

'All alone, are we?' he asked. I didn't like the way he was looking at me. I felt like a beetle in a jam jar. 'What are you doing here on your own?'

'Waiting for my father,' I said, my words coming out in a rasp. I couldn't look him in the eyes.

'Well, well. You're a lucky girl that I found you,' he said then. 'You see, your father's a friend of mine and he's asked me to come and get you. He's waiting at home with your tea.'

None of the deckchair man's words rang true and the worm of doubt that had been turning in the pit of my stomach now changed into a great big snake. I knew this man wasn't a friend of my dad's, and I knew my father wouldn't ever dream of giving me tea.

I wanted to run then, but I didn't. The big, empty beach, and the thought of being left there alone at night, was more frightening to me than this sweaty old man with greasy strands of hair pasted over his bald head. I didn't know then what he might do to me, but knew instinctively that it wasn't safe to be with him.

The deckchair man grabbed my hand, not tightly at first, and started pulling me along with him. When I tried to wriggle free, he moved his grip to my wrist. He was walking briskly now, with a strange sort of intensity. The tide had left puddles in the rippled sand and every so often the man lifted me over them.

'We don't want your shoes to get wet, do we?' he said. I could feel his fingers worming their way under my knickers and touching me there. I started to struggle now but he was gripping me hard.

When we reached a more sheltered spot, the deckchair man stopped walking and pushed me down onto the sand behind some rocks. I fought as hard as I could, but he was too big. It hurt and I cried, but he just carried on, not saying anything but making a horrid grunting noise. At some point he collapsed on my body, still now, and his hoarse breathing and the pounding of my heart drowned out the sound of the gulls and the waves on the shore.

Afterwards, he tried to do up the buttons of my dress, but he did them all wrong. He wasn't looking at me now.

'That wasn't too bad now, was it?' he said. 'You be a good girl and go back and wait for your father. He'll be along soon.' He handed me a bar of Cadbury's chocolate.

I stumbled back up the beach, my dress all torn and wet. As I reached the steps, I saw two girls coming down and I shoved the bar of chocolate into one of their hands. I pushed past them, feeling a desperate need to hide. Ahead of me, I saw a bus shelter and ran to it. I crouched there on the wooden bench, shivering with cold and shock, until Freda and my dad found me.

They didn't ask me what had happened, but simply tore me off a strip for messing my dress.

The rest of the week was hell for me. I couldn't tell anyone what had happened, but shook with fear every time I was taken down to the beach. Being left there again over the next three days was deeply traumatic. When it wasn't possible to melt into a crowd, I'd hide away in the bus shelter, trying to look as small and insignificant as I could, all the time sensing greedy, brutal eyes watching me, waiting to catch me on my own.

I never told anyone what had happened that day on the beach. When we got home, I buried my face in Gyp's fur and with every lick she gave me I felt a little less bruised inside. But the trauma of my rape would haunt me that long summer, and for years afterwards. Often, for no reason, I would find myself shaking uncontrollably. On my way to the library, or to the wash house, I'd feel watchful eyes on my back, and it was all I could do not to run. I didn't like being outside without Gyp at my side. At times, I thought I saw the deckchair man in a group of people on the street or in a shop, taking sneaky sideways looks at me, and then I'd want to run away and hide.

Whenever I caught a glimpse of myself in shop windows, I used to be really surprised that a normal kid looked back at me. I thought that I must be something so hideous for people to have treated me the way they had, like a piece of plasticine that's been pulled and twisted into an ugly blob; but here I was, an ordinary-looking child with brown hair in a clip. I couldn't recognize myself. So I would think, *There must be two of me, an outside person and an inside person.* And that got me thinking, *They don't know who I am. They have no idea.* And I realized then that I had to protect the inside person. They could beat the outside person as much as they liked. I knew me and I knew how I felt, and they didn't. *I'm going to have to look after the me in here.*

Chapter Eleven

I grew very fast that summer. It was almost as if the warm days had made me shoot up like a sunflower. I was still as thin as a whippet, but the backflips and head-stands I'd been practising had made me supple and strong. When I returned to Duke Street school in September, Mrs Jones made me move to a desk at the back as I was now one of the tallest in my form.

Being at the back of the class is usually the most covet-ed place, especially if you're a kid who's often picked on. However, for me it was a disaster. My eyes had been growing increasingly short-sighted over the past year, and now it was difficult to pick out the words and sums on the blackboard. I copied down what I thought I could see, but I often made mistakes.

By this time, we were old enough to use ink pens. All the kids in my class felt much more grown up now they had their own pen, but I found that I missed my pencil. The nib on my pen was old and splayed and sputtered ink all over my exercise book as I worked. Mrs Jones was fanatical about neatness. She used to walk up and down our rows of desks, watching what we were doing like some huge bird of prey. It was hard enough to work while her eyes were boring down on you; but when your pen nib just wouldn't behave, it was torture. My knuckles were constantly red from where she'd rapped them with her ruler.

Although I made many mistakes in class, my work was progressing well, largely due to with Miss Williams's lessons at Sunday School. I was so willing to learn, so keen to impress her, that my writing and drawing came on in leaps and bounds.

I was ten and a bit when my mother and sisters came back into my life. I had sensed that there was something wrong and that Freda and my dad were rowing more than usual. Usually, they sat in frigid silence in the evening after Dad had come in from work. She'd darn his socks while he read the paper, and it seemed like rarely a word ever passed between them. For the past few months, though, my father's fuse had been especially short, and Freda was as jumpy as a cat. I realized that the rows had something to do with his divorce and that Mum's solicitor had managed to track him down; but I didn't glean much because I hid in my room most of the time, keeping out of harm's way.

The full reason for my dad's behaviour became clear to me one day when he called me downstairs.

'You're going to your mother's tomorrow,' he said. 'You've got to go every Sunday and you'd better not put a foot out of line, my girl, or I'll give you such a hiding.'

My heart gave a great jump in my chest and for a minute I couldn't breathe. *She's found me. She wants me back!*

Dad turned then to Freda. 'Dress her in her Sunday best, and make sure she's tidy. I don't want that bitch saying we're not looking after her properly.'

It took me ages to get to sleep that night. It had been seven years since I'd last seen my mother and sisters. I wondered what it would be like when I saw them again. Would they hug me? Had they missed me at all? Might they even fight to keep me?

The next day, my father took me down to Victoria Bus Station. When we got there, a tall fair-haired girl was waiting for us. I instantly recognized Dora, but was shocked that she wasn't the four-year-old sister I remembered. I sensed there was little recognition on her part. She looked tense and I realized that seeing Dad after all these years must be a big shock to her. He greeted her tersely, showing no warmth at all. As far as he was concerned she was part of the enemy camp, one of my mother's spies.

'Get her back on the five o'clock bus. I don't want to be hanging round here waiting.' With that, Dad turned and left and we got on the bus together without a word.

Sitting on the top deck of the bus with Dora was excruciatingly awkward. She didn't say a single word to me, and I certainly wasn't able to start any sort of conversation with her. I wouldn't have had a clue what to say. Every minute of the journey was painful, and it was obvious we were both relieved when it was over.

Mum and Paddy had been given a bigger house than ours by the council. It was semi-detached and I knew if Freda could see it she'd have been spitting with envy. Dora led me down the side passage and through the back door into the kitchen. Mum was standing at the sink and wiped her hands on her pinny when she saw me. She was much older-looking than I remembered, and the lines around her mouth and eyes weren't happy ones; her face was scored with the marks of discontent and worry.

'Hello Judy,' she said. 'I see Dora found you then.'

Her movements looked somehow leaden, and forced. She came over and held me for a moment, but it was a strange, stiff sort of hug. I sensed that she was determined to play the motherly role as well as she could but that she'd never really known how, so it felt very uncomfortable to her. And if Mum felt awkward, I felt doubly so. She seemed like a stranger but it was as though something, some loving bond, was expected of us both and neither of us knew how to create it. I didn't know how to be chatty and outgoing; I was too used to hiding away. I must have seemed a charmless, wooden sort of girl to them.

I could see Mum had made an effort as the kitchen table had been laid with a cloth and plates of sandwiches and cake. But everything about that day had a strange formality that didn't make it comfortable for any of us. She took me through to the front room, where my three other sisters were sitting on the settee. The scene looked almost staged, and I sensed that the whole thing had been set up for my benefit. Mum introduced me to Mary and to my two half-sisters, Lily and Rose, and they said hello quietly and politely. It felt horribly awkward to have such a stilted first meeting with Mary. I wanted to say, *Don't you remember me? Your little sister, who you used to hold in your arms, wash and feed? Have you forgotten that?*

As the day wore on, I realized that Mum was desperate to create a perfect family picture that I could take home with me to taunt my father with. And I knew that he wanted to rile her too. He had drummed into me on our way to the bus station that I must paint a rosy picture of my life in Wood Street. It was obvious that, although my parents were now divorced, they were still obsessively locked in their own private dance, full of anger, revenge and competitiveness. And, as usual, I was just a pawn in their own selfish game. That was the reason Dad had taken me in the first place, retrieved me from the orphanage and continued to keep me. He just couldn't let Mum win.

My sisters had obviously been told that they couldn't go out with their friends, or disappear to play their usual games, and I sensed their feeling of resentment as we all sat in the front room.

'You'd better go and play in the garden with Judy,' Mum said after a few minutes. 'I'll call you in when it's tea.'

The girls sullenly trooped off, with me following. As soon as we got outside, however, they relaxed a bit and after a while they began to play a game. I stood back, watching from the sidelines. Mary hadn't come with us into the garden. At sixteen, she wanted to be off doing her own thing and it was clear that she wasn't interested in getting to know me.

I saw my mother and sisters once a month through the winter. I'd hoped that the more they got to know me the more they'd want me to be with them as part of the family. Things certainly began to get easier; I still found it impossible to join in the chit-chat around the table, but at least my sisters became more relaxed around me. Occasionally, though, if one of them got a bit mouthy, my mother would shoot a warning look and I'd know that they were still walking on eggshells in case I reported back that my sisters were being badly brought up.

As I got more familiar with the family, I started to see everything wasn't all that rosy at Malvern Grove. I noticed that Mum was usually careful around Paddy, and I sensed that the charming, brawny Irishman she'd fallen for had turned out feckless and difficult to manage, especially when he'd been drinking. When he came home after we'd had our tea, it was plain from his behaviour that he didn't want me in the house. He never spoke to me or looked my way. He simply acted as if I wasn't there, and gave everyone else grief by stomping about the house and slamming doors. He was never very nice to Mary and Dora, and I saw he treated Lily and Rose very differently to them.

You can't have had an easy time of it, I thought. *But at least you had each other.*

One day, a couple of weeks before Christmas, Mum came up to me whilst I was putting on my coat to go home.

'Here, Judy,' she said, 'I want you to have this.'

She took hold of my wrist and fastened a watch around it. Although she was as brusque as usual, I could sense something, like a little tendril of affection, stretch out and touch me.

'Happy Christmas, dear,' she said and patted my shoulder.

I felt then, for the first time, that Mum *had* wanted to see me again. She wasn't just being driven by the desire to be a thorn in my father's side. But, whether because of Paddy's bullying or her own feelings of guilt – or both – she hadn't felt capable of doing anything about it. And once she did have me back, she hadn't known quite what to do to make amends to the child who'd been torn from the family.

I wished then that I could have told my mother everything: how my dad and Freda had treated me, about the deckchair man, and how unhappy I'd been at home. But I knew I'd never dare. She'd only spill the beans to Dad, and then I'd get into the most terrible trouble. It was hard having secrets that I couldn't share. I was afraid that too much would come tumbling out if I did share them, and then I might get beaten to death for it.

When I got home that evening, I went up to my room and took the watch out of my pocket. It had fallen off on my way to the bus – it had a faulty clasp and was much too big for me. I realized it must have been an old one of Mum's that she didn't wear any more. I sat for a long time on my bed, looking at the watch in the palm of my hand. It felt such a precious thing, and I just wanted to hold it forever. As soon as I heard Freda's footsteps on the stairs, though, I quickly stuffed it into a sock and hid it away. I knew that if she ever found out I treasured anything she'd do her best to destroy it, as she always had.

My dad and Freda didn't celebrate Christmas like other families. We never had a tree, and there were no cards or decorations about the place. We didn't sit down together for Christmas lunch or give each other presents either. It was just an ordinary day, the same as any other.

The previous Sunday, Miss Williams had asked if I'd like to come with her while she went round to the poorer folk's houses – people who had lost someone in the war or who had undergone some other hardship – to give out hampers of food and toys. I loved being out on the dark streets beside her. She looked almost jaunty in her little pillbox hat, red nose peeping out over the folds of her scarf, as we walked along together in the smoggy night air, the bitter smell of coal smoke tinged with burning rubber from the Dunlop tyre factory.

I gazed through the windows of those houses we passed where the curtains hadn't yet been drawn to see strings of Christmas cards hanging on the walls and Christmas trees, twinkling all over, with presents piled up underneath. Whilst I thrilled to see them, I couldn't help but wish I had a home where there was a present under the tree waiting for me to open, a stocking bulging at the foot of my bed, and a family who loved me.

Chapter Twelve

Over the previous months, I'd noticed that my dad and Freda had been making more frequent visits to the Rippons, the wealthiest members of their Spiritualist circle. I sensed that my father was cooking something up but didn't know what. He and Freda were always whispering and scheming on the days we visited and, before we left the house, Dad used to spend more time than usual picking imaginary specks off his cream suit and tying extra flourishes in his cravat with long, perfectly manicured fingers. You would never know from his pale, soft hands that he worked in a factory.

Alec Rippon was a white-collar worker, an engineer in Manchester, and he and his wife and daughter lived in a large Victorian house in the posh, leafy suburb of Prestwich. It seemed like a palace to me when I compared it with our two-up, two-down in Wood Street. Freda seemed a little cowed by its grandness but my father wasn't one to act humbly, cap in hand, around the Rippons; and although the difference in social status between our families was huge, he always played his Christ Almighty role to the full.

Alec Rippon believed that he had the healing gift and had dreams of his own. Unlike my dad, he was a sincere man who genuinely wanted to help other people. As was usual in the Spiritualist church, he'd been assigned to a master – my father – to help him develop his powers. At the end of his training, he'd have to take some exams set by the National Spiritualist Union. My father set out to dazzle his apprentice, sensing that here was a lamb worth fleecing.

The Rippons' shiny, blue front door opened into a large porch as big as our front room. An umbrella stand stood next to the door, full of ivory topped canes. Freda, clearly both jealous and cowed by the grandness of it all, made me take my shoes off.

The porch opened onto a large carpeted hall. It was the first time I'd been in a house with fitted carpets – everyone I knew had lino on the floor. Against the wall next to the stairs stood a grandfather clock with a gleaming gold face, and on the walls hung big oil paintings of hunting scenes. I'd read about houses like this before in my Noel Streatfeild books, places where there were servants and nannies, and nurseries with rocking horses.

I was too young to be flustered by the grandness of the Rippons' house, but Freda always seemed on edge when we visited. Her lipstick looked a bit too red next to Gladys Rippons' powdered elegance. She used to rub it on her cheeks too, calling it rouge, and I saw now that her whole look seemed brash and common compared to Gladys.

The Rippons had turned one of the many rooms downstairs into a healing surgery where my father could receive patients. Alec stood by as Dad's assistant and Freda would act as nurse.

When patients arrived, they'd be ushered into a separate waiting room before Gladys showed them into the surgery. My father sat at the desk, a row of files on the shelf behind him, and, in his best doctor's voice, would ask the person to sit down while he questioned them about their problem. He would then show Alec how to use his hands correctly and cradle their head in the right way.

Whilst the surgery or evening seances were going on, I'd be sent off to play in the nursery with Cathleen, the Rippons' daughter, who was three years younger than me. She was an only child, and very spoilt. I don't think she liked me coming over, and if I picked up anything in her doll's house she'd stick out her lower lip in a pet and say, 'That's mine!' She certainly wasn't the kind of person I could play Tommies and Jerries with.

One evening, Cathleen showed me a board mounted on the wall in the kitchen. On it was a row of little bells and next to each was inscribed the name of a room in the house. She explained it was so that the servants knew where to go to when they were called to put coals on the fire or bring in a cup of tea.

'We don't have any servants, though, except for Mandy, who's our daily,' Cathleen said. 'So we don't use the bells at all.'

I thought of my mum, who'd been a maid at the house of a wealthy Spiritualist before she met Dad, and wondered if she'd had to wear a uniform and listen out for the bell ringing.

'How about we play at being mistress and maid,' I asked Cathleen. 'You can be my maid, if you like.'

I liked pretending to be mistress of the house, grandly ordering Cathleen around.

'Ah, Kitty, there you are,' I said, waving an imperious hand from the sofa. 'Go and fill the coal scuttle. I think I've got a chill coming on.'

'What do I do next?' Cathleen asked, not finding it as easy as me to slip into role play.

'Curtsy, like this,' I showed her how to bob. 'And say, "Yes'm". Then pretend to scoop coal out of the scuttle and put it on the fire.'

We started again and Cathleen managed her bob. After she pretended to put the coal on the fire, I showed her how to bring in the tea and pour it, picking imaginary sugar lumps from a bowl with tongs. At first, she sulked a bit, whining that she wanted to be the lady of the house, but she soon got into the game. I was getting an enormous kick out of our exchange of positions. In real life, Cathleen had the lovely home and the pretty manners, while I was the one who had to lug coal buckets in from the yard with raw hands every morning.

Things went on pretty much the same through the spring and summer of 1956, and then everything started to change. It was as if an earthquake was causing the foundations of my life to crack and its walls to fall in around me.

One day, my father called me downstairs and told me to sit down at the table.

'You're going to write a letter to your mother,' he told me, pushing paper and pencil at me. 'Do it now.'

He then started to dictate what he wanted me to write. 'Dear Mother,' he said. I wrote the words.

'I've decided that I want to live with my father permanently from now on,' he went on.

My hand stopped what it was doing and my pencil fell to the table. I couldn't go on.

Dad picked up the pencil, eyes snapping with anger, and forced it into my hand. 'Write it!' he shouted. 'Just do what I say!'

I still mutely refused, but my hand had started to tremble. Dad took my ear and twisted it viciously. 'Go on, do it. Now!'

He repeated the words and I started to write. The letters were shaky as I couldn't quite still my hand from its trembling.

'And I don't want to visit you or my sisters any more,' he went on. I wrote the words, tears trickling down my face.

'My school work is taking up so much time that I would rather be at home on Sundays to do it.' Dad let go of my ear once I'd finished that sentence. 'Just sign your name at the bottom,' he said, 'and then it's done.'

I signed my name, and it felt like I was signing my death warrant. And as my father sealed and addressed the envelope, I knew that the letter would indeed be a death blow to my dreams of getting to know my sisters and of finding an escape from my intolerable life with him and Freda.

After this, we didn't hear any more from my mother. Whether she was gearing up to fight for her right of access through her solicitor at that point, I don't know. All I thought then was that she must have believed what my letter said and had given up on me.

In September I went to a new school. North Hulme was closer to home and bigger than Duke Street Primary, and it felt like another huge change. Like any child moving up to senior school, I strained to keep up in that first few weeks. I now had lots of different teachers and had to find my way to a whole new set of classrooms; but I was used to looking after myself and managed to get along better than some.

I soon realized that finding my way around and keeping up with the work weren't going to be the only challenges

I had to face. In the playground at breaktime there were some tough, older kids who loved to pick on the first years and who were quick to single out any oddballs or loners. It was in my second week that the trouble began.

We were playing rounders one afternoon, and when it came to my turn I hit the ball hard and one of the 'deeps' went running after it. I flew from base to base; but as I was about to get a rounder, the girl who was standing by third base put her foot out and sent me flying. I had just enough time to get up and stand by her base before the ball was thrown to her by one of her team.

After the girl had thrown the ball back to the bowler, she turned to me with a smirk. I was furious and before I could prevent myself I hissed at her, 'I'll get you after school for this.'

She looked me up and down with a sneer. 'Okay then, be at the Croft after school and I'll show you how sorry you'll be you ever said that.'

When I got back to my team, the girl next to me in the line whispered, 'What did you say to her?'

I told her what I'd said and she looked at me, wide-eyed. 'She's really tough. Blimey, I don't know how you dared.'

As the afternoon wore on, I realized from the flurry of whispering that I'd challenged one of the toughest bullies in the school. I knew all the other girls thought I was mad, bad, or both; but I also knew that if I backed out now I'd lose every chance I had of their respect. But I had one thing in my favour that no one realized: I was used to being bashed to a pulp, so I wasn't really frightened of being hurt. My fear was more about putting myself in the spotlight.

On my way back home from school, I went to the Croft and stood on that bombed out piece of wasteland, waiting for the girl to come. As soon as she arrived, with a gang of three or four of her friends, she pitched straight into me and I fell backwards onto the ground. I was up in a moment though and went for her, slapping, punching and pulling hair. We fought and scratched like wildcats until her nose started bleeding and she managed to pull out a chunk of my hair by the roots.

After a few minutes, it was clear to the girl that I wasn't going to give in, and so she backed off towards her group of friends. I stood there alone on the Croft, feeling bruised, but one hell of a lot better than after I'd had a hiding from my dad.

As I was turning to go, the girl tried to claw back some of her power, but it was half-hearted now. 'You watch it. You just watch it, girl, or I'm going to get you.' I didn't turn back to face her. I knew I'd won.

Aching all over, and covered in bruises and scratches, I went back home. I was shaking now with the stress of the fight and had to go and sit upstairs for a while, with my arms around Gyp, before I was ready to start my after-noon chores.

I thought that would be the end of it. What I hadn't bargained on was someone reporting the fight to the head-mistress. Once again I found the unwelcome glare of the spotlight upon me in assembly the next morning.

The headmistress spoke sternly. 'Last night there were two girls fighting on the Croft. You all know perfectly well that this is totally unacceptable behaviour.' She glared round the hall at the five hundred-odd pupils.

'Would those two girls stand up, please. You know who you are.'

For some reason, I didn't at once click that the head was referring to our fight – to me. I looked around the room for a moment. Then I saw the girl I'd been fighting stand up and the penny dropped.

As I stood up too, feeling very small and not at all victorious now, I didn't know what to do with my legs, my arms, my mouth – any part of me. I felt so self-conscious and afraid that I ended up putting my hands on my hips – they felt so awkward that I had to put them somewhere. I sensed the headmistress freeze, and saw the shock on the faces of the other teachers. I then realized that I'd only managed to look defiant. They must have been surprised that this quiet kid, who always sat at the back of the class and finished her work without any trouble, wasn't the girl they'd supposed she was.

'I want you both outside my office straight after assembly,' the head went on to say. 'And the rest of you remember, I simply won't tolerate fighting at the school.'

I got the strap that day, but at least the fight ensured that I had no more trouble from any of the other girls. They still weren't particularly friendly, but I knew they had some respect for me now.

School wasn't the only big change in my life that autumn. I noticed that the whisperings and rows emanating from Dad and Freda's bedroom at night were becoming more frequent as the weeks passed. More often than not, they coincided with a trip to the Rippons' house. Neither of them bothered to tell me what was going on, but I watched and I listened.

The first thing that happened was that Freda gave up her cleaning job and started busying herself around the house and packing things away in boxes. I came home one afternoon to find that the piano had gone.

Friends from my dad's Spiritualist circle started popping

round over the following weeks to pick up pieces of furniture, the sewing machine, and boxes of kitchen stuff.
Once, when I was upstairs in my room, I heard Freda
let someone in and I decided to pry on their conversation.
I quietly walked half way down the stairs and sat there
listening hard.

'So when are you off, Freda?' the woman asked.

'We don't know yet,' she replied. 'But we're looking forward to the weather in Australia, although I hope it'll be
bearable for us.'

'Well, a nice change from the drizzle and smog here.
I must say, I do envy you.'

'Well, it won't be easy, but at least Jack has a business for
him when he gets there. He'll be running a fleet of taxis.'

'Good for him, and good for you. I do wish you all the
luck,' the woman said. I sensed then that she was moving
to get her coat, and so I nipped back up to my room.

After that, Freda started telling the milkman, the paperboy, and the shopkeepers the same story. I found it strange,
as she was usually very slow in coming forward with
information she considered to be nobody's business but
her own. The reason, however, became clear to me one
evening while I was playing with Cathleen.

'We're getting ready to move to Australia,' I told her.

'No you're not. You're going to South Africa,' she
answered. 'And we're going too.'

'But I've heard my mother tell everyone,' I said.

'It's not right,' she insisted doggedly. 'My mother
showed me South Africa on the map, and we're definitely
going there.'

I went silent then, sensing that she was telling the truth
and that Freda and my dad had been spinning their usual
web of lies, preparing in advance to cover their tracks.

It was now the beginning of December and I was feeling very jumpy. Not knowing when we were going, and even whether I'd be taken along, was making me nervous. Freda had already told me I was no longer allowed to go to Sunday School, and I was very upset that I wouldn't have a chance to say goodbye to Miss Williams. She must have been wondering if I was ill, or if something had happened to me. I hated to think of her buying the fairy cakes for our tea and then finding that I hadn't bothered to turn up .

One afternoon, after I got back from school, Freda took me down to the hairdressers on City Road.

'Can you cut her hair?' she asked. 'I want it all off, as short as possible.'

The hairdresser raised an enquiring eyebrow. Girls never wore their hair like that.

Freda was quick with her explanation. 'They've all got nits at school, and I don't want her catching them.'

I wondered why Freda was doing this and why she was bothering to lie. Up until now, she'd always cut my hair herself, so why was she forking out on a hairdresser? And her story about the nits was complete nonsense. The nit nurse, whom we used to call Nitty Nora, hadn't visited our classroom in months, and it was a while since we'd had an outbreak. You always knew when a kid was discovered with nits because all the girls wore these pointy wool hats in class to keep their hair safe, and the boys came in with hardly any hair at all.

I was given a boy's crew cut and after we got home, I went upstairs and sat on the floor, feeling the shorn ends with my fingers and feeling horribly naked. *What will people say when they see me?* I thought to myself.

I felt even more self-conscious when Freda made me try on a pair of jeans, a thin checked jersey, and a cotton windjammer jacket. It was clear to me that my father and Freda had decided to dress me as a boy, although at that stage I didn't know the plan they had cooked up, a plan that included their taking me out of the country, making sure they covered their tracks and giving my mother, her lawyer and the welfare people the slip.

'Why do I have to wear these?' I asked her.

She was abrupt. 'Just do as you're told. You're going to need them for the cold weather.'

All the rest of my clothes were bundled up and given away. When I got back from school, I found my bed had gone and that all my things, including Susie, my books, and the watch my mother had given me, had been put in carrier bags in the front room.

I went to Freda and begged her, 'Can't I just keep my bear?'

She turned on me sharply. 'Stop being such a baby,' she said. 'No, you bloody can't.' She cuffed me out of the way. 'Now just get lost. Can't you see I've got enough to do without listening to you whinging?'

I went and sat upstairs forlornly, not realizing that the worst was yet to come.

The house was all packed up now and the rooms were bare of everything except a few suitcases. My dad was home, as he too had left his job by now, and I stayed out of his way, knowing that the slightest thing would set him off. I was upstairs with Gyp when he called me.

'Judy! Get Gyp down here. Now!'

Gyp pricked up her ears when she heard her name and got off the bed, thinking she might be in for some scraps. She trotted eagerly out of the room and I followed her, catching her up in my arms, sensing that something was amiss.

Two men were standing at the bottom of the stairs with my father. One of them beckoned me down.

'Here, give her to me.' I went up to him and he took Gyp out of my arms. He held her like he thought she might bite him. Gyp gave a whine and tried to struggle out of his grasp, but I just stood there, frozen in horror. I wanted to ask them why they were taking Gyp, but I didn't make a sound.

Neither my dad nor the two men looked my way, but one of them must have sensed my anguish. He stood awkwardly, and began clearing his throat. 'Righto. We'll be off then,' he said.

Gyp was looking at me with such piteous eyes that I sprang forward, darting round my father to follow the men. They were walking now across the cobbles towards their van, holding the struggling dog tightly. Inside it, I saw other dogs looking out through the glass from behind an iron grill. They started barking when they saw Gyp, who just cowered as one of the men opened the back of the van and the other shoved her inside.

I stood outside in the road, wanting to whimper and howl myself; but I made no sound as I saw the van pull away. Gyp's pleading eyes never left my own, and they burned themselves into my soul.

After Gyp went, I didn't really care what happened to me. I moved about the house listlessly, feeling dead inside. The only time I felt that a part of me was still living was when my thoughts turned to Gyp, and then the pain cut through me like a knife. That night, as I lay on my bedroom floor, it felt like my heart was being ripped from my chest, and scalding tears poured down my face.

In the middle of the night, I was shaken awake by Freda. 'Get your clothes on,' she said. 'We're going.'

I hurried to put on the boys' clothes I'd been given to wear and left my room to join her and my dad downstairs. He was loading suitcases into a van outside. There was snow on the ground.

'Get in the back, and not a sound from you,' Dad said, grabbing me by the collar and pushing me into the back of the van. 'And don't put your head anywhere near the window.' There was barely room for me to lie down among the cases but I did as I was told.

I heard Freda and my dad get in the front and we moved off down the street. It was freezing on the bare metal floor and I had nothing I could use as a pillow, and no blanket to keep me warm. Every bone in my body protested as the van bounced over the cobblestones.

At some point along the way, it suddenly occurred to me that maybe I wasn't being taken with my dad and Freda to South Africa. After all, there wasn't a suitcase for me, and all my things had been destroyed or given away.

They're going to dump me beside the road somewhere, I thought, panic-stricken. *What will I do? Where will I go?*

But the van didn't stop, except once, after a few hours, when we drew up at a transport café. My father opened the doors at the the back of the van.

'Get out,' he said. I sat up and scrambled out of the van. I was so cold and stiff I thought my legs would buckle under me. I couldn't feel my feet at all.

Dad took me to the men's toilet and made me go in with him, to my shame. 'Just remember,' he said. 'If anyone asks you, your name isn't Judy. It's Sprig.'

I wasn't allowed to have a hot drink or anything to eat with the others at the transport café. My father didn't want anyone seeing me with them so I was bundled straight back into the van.

By the time we reached Southampton, I was starving and hugely relieved to get out of the van. It was an icy morning and there was a mist over the sea. There was a large ship at the dockside and I guessed we'd be going on it. I stood there in the cold as my dad unloaded the van, thinking bleakly that any chance I might have had to get to know my mum and sisters had now gone. They'd just forget me like they had before.

In the customs hall, a big hangar-like building, Freda and my Dad caught sight of the Rippons and went over to them. Cathleen had told me that her parents planned to set up a healing sanctuary in South Africa and I had guessed the rest – that my father had sold the idea to Alec and was preparing to sponge off him mercilessly. I don't know what story he'd concocted for the Rippons to explain my being dressed as a boy, but they didn't seem surprised. Cathleen couldn't help staring, though, and her mother nudged her with a reproving look.

The customs officials were all sitting at long white tables along one side of the room. My father and Freda told me to stay with the Rippons and then queued up to have their papers stamped. I saw Dad turn and point at me and the customs man nod. I could just detect a tension in my father's shoulders, knowing that an official in uniform was the one thing certain to unnerve him.

All of a sudden, I had a frantic urge to shout out loud, feeling the desperate sort of courage that comes when it's your very last chance. *Don't let them take me! Stop them taking me! I don't want to go!* But Dad and Freda were waved through and the moment was gone. The breath stuck in my throat, my cry a silent one.

As we went up the gangway, Mrs Rippon handed me a bag of clothes my father must have asked her to bring along for me. I wondered again what she really knew.

Chapter Thirteen

Once on board the *Bloemfontein Castle,* we parted from the Rippons and my father led Freda and me down stairwell after stairwell to the bowels of the ship to find our cabin. Our ten-pound immigration ticket, paid for by the Rippons, afforded us a cell-like cubby hole, below the waterline, which smelt of damp. There were two bunks for Dad and Freda, and a tiny camp bed for me along the facing wall behind the door. On a small chest of drawers against the other wall was a tray with a pitcher of water and two glasses. There was barely a body-width between the beds.

I sat on my bed while Dad and Freda unpacked their cases in silence. When my father had finished putting his things away, he straightened up and turned to me. He was so tall that he had to bend his head so it didn't hit the ceiling.

'Right,' he said. 'Let's get a few things straight. On board this ship you're to do exactly what I say and follow my rules.' He proceeded to list them.

'First, you're not leaving my sight. And you'll stay in the room unless I tell you to come with me.

'Second, you're to use the boys' toilet and you're to go only when I say you can.

'Third, you're not to talk to anybody. If you want to go anywhere at all, you ask me.

'If I see you doing one thing out of line, you'll be locked in the cabin. Remember that. You will not disobey me.'

I nodded but couldn't force myself to meet his eyes, which were cold and expressionless. I felt panicked that there wasn't any place for me to hide. Even shrunk back against the wall, as far as I could get from my father, I felt he was still near enough to me to feel his breath on my skin.

Outside the cabin, I could hear the excited voices of a party of other passengers. I sensed briefly what it must feel like to be in their shoes, setting out on the biggest adventure of their lives. But it was only for a moment, and then my world closed in on me again and I was back in the cabin, full of horror at being trapped in this tiny space with my abusers, and feeling nothing but a horrible sense of forboding.

We were stranded in port, fogbound, for three days and my father was growing jumpier by the minute. I knew the court had given my mum the right to see me and that taking me out of the country without their permission would get my dad into no end of trouble if he was caught. He didn't let me out of his sight for a moment, and I knew he must have been nervous that at any moment officials might board the ship and arrest him.

Once we were under way, however, he relaxed a bit and I was allowed to spend time in the library on my own. It was there, only a couple of days into our voyage, that I found a book containing a list of the passengers on board. I cast my eyes over it idly, looking for our names. The Rippons were there, but nothing under 'R' for Richardson.

Then I saw an odd thing: there was an entry for a Mr Jack and a Mrs Freda Riccardos and their twelve-year-old son.

It was strange that I didn't put two and two together – after all it was clear that Freda had dressed me as a boy and that now I had to be called Sprig, not Judy; but when I saw the words on the page I was simply confused. I couldn't begin to understand why I'd been logged in as Freda's son.

It was then that I made a big mistake, and one that was going to cost me dearly. I ran into the lounge, where my father was sitting reading a paper.

'They've made a mistake! They've put me down as your son,' I said to him.

Dad's reaction was as instant as a snake uncoiling itself to strike. He sprang out of the leather armchair and grabbed my arm so brutally that I gave a little cry. He dragged me out of the lounge and down several flights of stairs to the lower deck. I stumbled several times but didn't fall. Once inside our cabin, he locked the door and kicked me so hard that I fell, sprawled half on, half off, my bed.

'As you didn't obey my orders ...' he slapped me across my face, 'I'm going to lock you in.' He shook me by the throat, squeezing my windpipe so I couldn't breathe. 'And then you can bleat all you like. No one will hear you.'

Dad let me go then and I instantly curled up into a ball. I waited for more blows, but they'd stopped coming. Then I heard my father opening a drawer and taking something out of it.

What's he doing now? I thought in panic. *What's he getting? What's he going to do to me?* Then I heard the scratch of his pen on paper and a couple of minutes later he paused.

'Come here.' Dad's voice was steely. The red heat of his earlier temper had eased, but his mood had moved to one of ice-cold sadism. What I didn't know then was that this mood would last, unbending, for weeks and that I was to suffer like a moth struggling on a pin throughout the whole voyage.

'Sign here,' he said, handing me the pen. Although the words were a blur, I managed to read them, despite a painful hammering in my head.

> *I will not go out of the cabin.*
> *The cabin door must always be locked.*
> *I can only use the men's toilets, and only when my father agrees.*
> *I can only go to breakfast and dinner with my father.*
> *I will speak to nobody.*

I signed the paper, which my father folded and put away. 'Lock the door,' he said coldly as he left the room.

The next day, as I lay on my camp bed, I felt as if the horrid fetid hole that had become my cell was closing in around me. I could hear nothing; I had nothing to look at except blank walls, and the closed-off porthole was some-how the more awful for its being there. I'd rather have had a blank wall than the suggestion of a window onto the outside. What air there was seemed to get thinner by the hour, and the water in the jug was chlorinated and tasted horrible.

I really think I might go mad.

Then, as the day wore on, I became aware of a change in the sea's motion. It was definitely getting choppier. When Freda and my father came down to dress for dinner, they moved carefully round the cabin, looking as though they were trying to keep their breathing steady.

'I'm not feeling great, Jack,' Freda said a bit weakly. 'Now we've entered the Bay of Biscay, they say it mightn't let up for days.'

The dining room was half empty that evening. I noticed that the waiters had raised flaps on the tables to stop the plates and cutlery slipping off onto the floor. The diner sitting opposite me gave a laugh when salt cellars and glasses slid at speed across the table as the boat plunged down into the trough of a wave. But mostly, people were quiet: the usual chattering enthusiasm for the voyage had waned that evening, and most of the passengers' faces wore a strange expression, as if they were concentrating hard. I realized that they were willing themselves not to throw up.

By morning, there were ropes tied in the stairwells and along the corridors as makeshift handrails, to stop people from being thrown to the floor. When I left the cabin to go to the toilet, I saw that people had been sick in the passage. I'd heard them retching in the night and some of them obviously hadn't made it to the bathroom. When I got back, Freda and my father were sitting up in bed, looking a bit green.

'Go and fetch us some soda water and dry toast,' Freda said to me. 'There's no way I can move.'

I couldn't believe my luck. As the day wore on, I had to do various bits of fetching and carrying but was pretty much free to wander the ship at will. My father didn't seem to have the strength to make me keep to his rules; in fact it was quite clear he and Freda wanted me out of their way. My presence only caused them extra irritation.

Luckily, I didn't feel sick at all and soon found my way outside to the fresh air, holding tight to the rope banisters as I climbed the flights of stairs to the upper deck. Once out there, I staggered up the ship to the bows, clinging onto the rail for dear life. I now felt like the sprig they'd named me: a fragile stem being torn and buffeted by the gale.

If any of the crew had seen me out on deck I would have got soundly ticked off. I could easily have been swept overboard. Huge splashes were coming over the sides of the ship, and the crash of the waves as they hit the bows was deafening. As I stood there, tossed and blown almost to pieces, I felt exultant as the clean, heady oxygen filled my lungs, invigorating every vein and nerve in my body. After the stifling, dank airlessness of the cabin, the freedom to wander about on deck was like a cool drink of water to a wanderer in the desert.

I stood there alone, clinging to the rail, and facing into the wind, a small figurehead amidst a vast and boiling sea. I knew that it wasn't just the air invigorating me. I felt at one with the storm, a part of it – wild and lost.

It was after the Bay of Biscay that my nightmare really began.

The sea became calm, and the sun grew hotter. The other passengers started at last to enjoy the trip, sunning themselves on deck and cooling off in the pool. I'd watch them come in to dinner looking rosy and relaxed. But deep inside the ship the heat grew unbearable. Alone in my cabin, I started to wonder if I was going to die. No one would have guessed how bad it was for me down there in the middle of the day as the air had cooled down by the time people returned to their cabins to dress for dinner.

I lay on my bed in a stupor, dressed in my jeans and shirt. At times, I almost passed out, and once I was forced put my mouth to the keyhole in an attempt to suck air through it. My hair was wringing wet and I had little to drink as our pitcher of foul-tasting water was only changed once a day. I used a little of it to wet a flannel to put over my face, but it didn't bring my temperature down for long and soon grew warm.

Sometimes my heart started pounding and fluttering at a frightening pace, and then I started to feel really panicky. Overheated and starved of oxygen, I felt terribly alone. There was nobody else on our deck, no footsteps, or any other sounds at all. If I had cried out and pounded my fists on the door, no one would have heard.

After a few days of this torture, I felt desperate enough to ask my father if I could have the door open.

'No, you can't. You know the rules,' he said, glaring at me.

I was sure that's what he would say, but I had to try. I knew that he felt safer if the door was locked. That way nobody would discover there was anyone in the cabin.

Every day I longed for dinner time. My dad must have decided that he'd better let me eat with the other passengers or people might question my absence. As it was, I did wonder what the Rippons thought. Cathleen must surely have told them that I was never in the playroom with the other kids, and didn't join in the games on deck; but they never said anything. In those days, children weren't encouraged to join in the conversation at mealtimes, so people didn't think to ask me anything, and it didn't seem strange to them that I never said a word.

As soon as dinner was over, I was always told to go straight back to the cabin. To put off the torture for a few minutes more, I used to chew each mouthful really slowly.

One afternoon, I heard footsteps in the corridor outside our cabin and the door was flung open. I sat up, startled. No one ever came down in the middle of the day. I saw my father standing there and instantly my mind started racing wildly. A rat in a trap.

Oh God, what have I done this time?

'Get up,' he said. 'Come with me.'

I followed him along the passage and up the flights of stairs to the deck. My eyes were dazzled by the sunlight and sparkling water. Everything was so brilliant and blue. I hadn't seen daylight for a week or more.

I wondered what was going on. I knew my dad wouldn't have let me out through pity. He'd never felt an ounce of the stuff in his life.

As we stepped forward towards the crowd that was gathered by the pool, the ship's captain beckoned us over. He was standing in front of a line of boys and girls who were wearing T-shirts with name tags pinned to them.

'Come on, slow coach, didn't you realize it was the Crossing of the Line Ceremony?' he said jovially. 'It's not every day you get to cross the Equator.'

In his hand, the captain was holding a list. I realized then that he must have been reading out all the kids' names and was now waiting to hand me my name tag. My father must have felt in a bit of a spot earlier when my name was called out and I wasn't there.

I took my name tag and pinned it to my shirt. I was conscious of everyone around me laughing and having a good time while my father stood in the midst of it all like a dark ghoul at a wedding party, fixing me with a glare as if to say, 'Don't you dare do anything to call attention to yourself.'

One by one, the kids were covered in a flour and water paste and thrown into the pool. When it was my turn, I turned away from my father's glaring eyes as paste was slapped on my shirt and in my hair, determined to have fun like the other kids. Then I was taken to the poolside. As one of the crew pushed me in the water, I felt an extraordinary sense of relief as the cool water closed in over my head before I came to the surface.

I felt in my element, playing team games in the pool. I'd learned to swim on our summer holidays while I was at St Joseph's and now I dived down confidently to fish rubber quoits from the bottom of the pool, as slick and bendy as a seal. And when it was my turn to walk along a wooden plank without falling in the water, I was as poised and able as a gymnast. Even though I was aware of my father and Freda standing by the pool with the other parents, pretending to enjoy the fun but looking hard-faced nonetheless, I loved every moment of it.

After about twenty minutes in the pool, it was time to get out. My father came straight to me. He didn't need to say a word – I knew my time was up and I felt as if a cloud had all at once covered the sun.

Why can't you just let me be? Just leave me for once to be a normal kid along with the others?

It was so oppressive having my jailer bearing down on me that I could almost bear going down to the cabin. At least I was out of his sight and I knew it wasn't long till dinner time.

When we docked at Freetown, in Sierra Leone, there was an excited buzz at breakfast. The passengers were getting a day out to explore and everyone shared in that feeling of escape. Everyone, that is, but me. I knew that I'd be left alone on board. My dad would never dare let me near another customs official if he could help it.

If I'd known that morning what I found out later – that back in England my mum had alerted the authorities about my abduction and that officials in Freetown were only a day away from being given the order to make me a ward of court – I would have jumped ship there and then. But I didn't know, and the order came after we'd already left port.

I found out later that Mary and Dora had been sent to Wood Street to deliver my Christmas present and that my mum, on hearing that we'd emigrated to Australia a couple of weeks before, had fallen into a huge fury that that my father had duped her. She immediately took action and told a journalist from the *Daily Mirror* about the abduction. They moved fast, printing the story with a picture of me, making enquiries at Australia House, and painstakingly searching every passenger list from air and sea lines. When they realized my father had left a false trail, they turned their attention to immigration ships leaving for other destinations. The Union Castle Line gave them the information they were searching for and the authorities were informed. All this happened quickly, but not quite quick enough to catch up with us at Freetown.

That evening, everyone came back from their trip ashore loaded down with scarves and trinkets, and at dinner the women leant over the table to admire the bangles and necklaces they'd bought in the market. Everyone was talking about the imminent Christmas party.

'We've managed to buy some really lovely material for Cathleen's fancy dress costume,' Gladys Rippon was saying. 'And it cost almost nothing. Although, goodness knows how I'm going to make it without a sewing machine.'

'Mum, am I going to have a stocking this year?' Cathleen asked her.

'Never you mind, cheeky. I expect Father Christmas might just have to come down one of the funnels.'

'But how's he going to find our cabin? And where are we going to put his glass of sherry and cake?'

Mrs Rippon and the other diners laughed indulgently. 'Oh, I expect he'll think of something, poppet. But you'd better be a good girl and eat your chicken or he might think better of it.'

I sat there quietly, soaking up the conversation, knowing that in our cabin there certainly wouldn't be a stocking hanging at the end of my bed. After all, Santa had never managed to track me down before, so he certainly wasn't likely to do so on board the *Bloemfontein Castle*.

I nursed a little hope that I might be able to join in with the other kids on Christmas Day. I'd never known that Christmas could be a time of such festivities. People had been talking about it for days. As well as a fancy dress party, the crew had organized a visit from Santa for the children. Christmas at the orphanage had just meant one thing – more chapel services; and at Wood Street, my dad and Freda used to spend most of the day at church. I didn't know it could be like this.

Although I'd hoped that this Christmas Day might be different, I wasn't surprised when my dad made me go down to the cabin after breakfast. As usual, there I stayed until dinner time. Lying there on my bed that day, the silence of the lower deck felt even more godforsaken than before. I knew that, out on deck, there would be games and celebrations all day long and felt a huge, hard lump in my throat.

When Freda came down to the cabin to dress for dinner, I watched her getting dolled up in a satiny gold dress she'd bought at the market. I thought it looked awful as it was slimy-looking and had puke-like swirls all over it. Once she'd finished putting on her make-up she put on a pair of matching gold slippers. I sat on the bed and thought to myself how incongruous it looked – this hard-faced, unsmiling woman wearing such a twinkly, girlish outfit, the lipstick on her cheeks making her look like a painted clown.

I don't think I'd ever seen Freda laughing. I don't think she knew how. She'd certainly never cracked a joke or giggled with her friends in my hearing. Over the years she'd been with my father, her mouth had hardened into a sour expression, with deep lines scored on either side. I wondered if her mouth was actually able to stretch itself into a laugh, even if it had wanted to. I guessed not.

As I looked across the table at Mrs Rippon at dinner, I realized that she and Freda would never be more than civil to each other. Freda didn't know how to be friends with anyone she couldn't patronize, and I knew she felt uncomfortable that Gladys was posher and more self-assured than she was. At home, Freda was in the habit of acting the role of spiritual do-gooder, doling out advice – and occasionally food – to the less well-off women in their Spiritualist circle. I used to watch how she acted with her friend Madge, patronizing her in a superior sort of way. It worked with Madge as she was always down on her luck. But with Gladys it was different, and Freda felt ill at ease around her.

My father had no such problem with the Rippons. While Freda sat at the table rather stiffly, he showed an easy familiarity with Alec and Gladys. Considering he was only a factory worker, it was amazing that he could be so charmingly confident around them. My dad had all the oily sociability Freda lacked, and I'm sure that's why she was drawn to him.

At Cape Town, the ship docked to let some of the passengers disembark and take on new supplies for the final leg of the trip to Durban. Once again, everyone was allowed on shore for the day and the mood was jubilant – especially as they'd at last reached the country that was to be their new home.

Breakfast was at six that day because the tour buses were due to leave earlier than usual. My dad told me I couldn't go back to the cabin until later, in case I was discovered on board after everyone else had left.

'The steward will have finished cleaning it in another hour so you can go down then,' he said. 'Wait in the dining room and then move when the coast is clear.'

I had no intention of doing what Dad told me that morning, so I waited until I knew he and Freda had left and then, instead of slipping down to the cabin, I went up on deck. The warm air smelt fresh and spicy and I breathed it in hungrily. Freedom felt so good that morning, and I revelled in it.

I was dazzled by the smells, the sounds, the colours of everything around me. On the dockside, native women in the most glorious clothes – rich magentas, greens and golds – had laid out carved animals, jewellery and scarves. I'd never seen anyone wearing that rich, deep orangey yellow colour before. In Manchester people wore only a few colours, and they were always drab and boring.

These woman had gleaming, dark skin and I thrilled to hear them shouting across at each other in a language I'd never heard before. Some of them had babies strapped on their backs, others were carrying baskets of yellow fruit on their heads. It was like one of my storybooks come to life. And it was as different to my life in the grey smoggy streets of Manchester as I could have imagined.

People were still streaming off the ship, and as I looked down at the gangway I saw a woman on her own, struggling with two kids and a pushchair. I knew I shouldn't speak to anyone but I found myself moving forward to help her anyway.

'Thank you, dear,' she said to me gratefully. 'If you wouldn't mind carrying my little girl, that would be a great help.'

When we reached the bottom of the gangway, I was about to turn and push my way back up when I felt a heavy hand on my shoulder. I spun round in panic.

'You wait here.' A man in uniform stood beside me, looking stern.

I almost gave a sob, feeling overwhelmed with panic.

I've got to get away. He'll find out who I am. My dad will kill me.

It never occurred to me that the man was simply holding me back so that I didn't get in the way of the other passengers. Instead, I was immediately convinced that I was going to be taken away and never seen again. My dad's horror of officials had rubbed off on me to the extent that I couldn't imagine any other scenario.

I knew I had to escape and cast around desperately for an opening in the crowd, but the people were still streaming down the gangway. *Come on! Hurry up!* I willed them to stop dawdling. Then I saw a gap and, giving a sharp wriggle, violently tore myself away from the man's grasp.

'Hey, you!' he shouted after me. 'What do you think ...?' But I didn't hear the rest of his words as I'd already gone.

I was convinced that the official would come after me in his heavy boots and that he might find me if I went down to the cabin. So instead I went down to the first-class deck and looked for a place to hide. I found a broom cupboard and sat there for hours in the dark. The smell of polish reminded me of St Joseph's.

Sometime in the afternoon, a steward opened the door to fetch a broom and nearly got the fright of his life when he saw me.

'What on earth do you think you're doing?' he said. 'You're a naughty boy, playing games in here and giving honest people a fright.'

I shrank back from his wagging finger.

'Now get lost. I don't want to see you again.'

I didn't need to be told twice and in a few seconds was back in our cabin. Lying in my prison cell was preferable to the beating I'd get from Dad if he discovered I'd been outside.

We finally reached Durban on 31 December 1956, after a journey of almost four weeks. During that time I had hardly left our dank and airless cabin. I felt an enormous sense of relief wash over me as I left my prison cell behind.

As I stood in the baking sun, outside on the dockside, I noticed a banner attached to the rails which read 'Happy New Year'. I wondered then what it would bring in this new land, full of possibilities.

Chapter Fourteen

*D*urban was blisteringly hot. I reckoned it was easily hotter than any day we'd ever had in Manchester. I stood on the station platform and looked around me. In the glare of the shimmering sunlight a host of lean black porters strode back and forth, carrying bags. They looked like glossy, ebony carvings, and I couldn't help feeling a buzz of excitement as I took in the scene.

My father was in his element, wearing a new khaki safari suit, the jacket tied at the waist with a belt. In his new suit and hat, I thought he looked like someone out of a Tarzan film, and I could tell he was really into the idea of himself as some sort of colonial grandee. As we had to carry our own bags, though, I'm sure everyone else recognized we were just steerage passengers on a ten-pound immigration ticket.

We stayed one night in Durban. As we walked to our hotel, along a street lined with palm trees, I thought how wonderful this wide avenue was after our narrow cobbled streets in Hulme. I was even more amazed to see that natives in costume were running along it, pulling brightly painted carts behind them. They were wearing huge headdresses and had tinkling bells around their ankles.

I heard Gladys Rippon explain to Cathleen that the little carriages on poles were called rickshaws. White people were sitting inside them, some of them dressed in safari suits like my dad's.

Next day we took a long train ride to Johannesburg. I spent the whole time looking out of the carriage window, marvelling at the scenery. I couldn't get over how wide and bright the sky was or how far the horizon stretched. In England I'd never seen the long edge of the sky as all the grey roofs and chimney pots, churchtowers and factory chimneys got in the way. Now, as I saw the bushveld in all its glory, the flat sandy expanse of it, the scrubby bushes and strange reddish mountain ridges in the distance, I felt very much alive.

We didn't arrive in Johannesburg until late in the evening. The warm night air smelt of flowers and spice. We passed through streets of white wooden houses encircled by verandas and finally came to the hotel we were to spend the night at, the Casa Mia. It seemed very grand to me. I had never had a bath with hot water coming out of the tap before and was very impressed. I spent as long as I could in it that night, topping it up with steaming water again and again until the hot ran cold.

The next day we took our bags further down the same road to our boarding house. The Allendene Residential Hotel wasn't half as impressive as the Casa Mia. In fact, it was pretty dilapidated. It was a typical refuge for poor white immigrant families in Berea, a decaying area of Johannesburg. We were shown to our room by the landlord, Mr Adams, who was a lardy, pasty-faced man with greasy strands of hair pasted over his bald head.

'Here you are, then,' he said. 'Tea's at six, breakfast between five-thirty and seven. Bath at the end of the corridor. Not to be used more than once a week for the kids.'

We put our cases down and looked around the room. I noticed that the window was cracked and stuck up with tape. The floor was bare wooden boards. Freda went over to the double bed and pulled back the cover. A couple of brown cockroaches skittered across the mattress. They must have been all of three inches long.

'Bloody hell, Jack,' she sighed. 'This place is a bit of a dump.'

My father just ignored Freda and, with his back to her, began to unpack his suits and shirts and hang them in the wardrobe.

'Just remember who's paying the rent,' he reminded her curtly, without turning round. 'And don't go shouting your mouth off about it and moaning to Gladys and Alec.'

To give them their due, the Rippons didn't make a single complaint themselves when we all collected downstairs in the dining room later. The general scruffiness of the Allendene must have seemed a shocking change for them – a far cry from their comfortable Victorian house back home in Manchester. Gladys was definitely tougher than her manicured hands and carefully applied make-up would lead you to imagine. She had clearly resolved to support Alec one hundred per cent in his mission to do Christ's duty. I'd always thought, with her posh voice like a teacher's, that Gladys was like royalty. Now I was even more impressed by her.

At one point, a cockroach scuttled across our table and I saw Gladys's eyes flicker. Cathleen let out a small squeal.

'Shush, Cathleen,' her mother admonished her. 'Just remember what I said.'

This is what God has meant me to learn, I read in her eyes. *We have to do these things, even when it's hard.*

After tea, I went outside. In the hour or so before it got dark I wandered about the streets nearest the Allendene. The houses in Berea had obviously been built in better times and although they were dilapidated now, I still thought they looked very grand. The large wooden bungalows had elegant verandas at the front and their gardens were full of exotic trees and shrubs. All along the roadside were heaps of blossom, little mauve trumpet-shaped flowers, that had fallen from the trees.

In Hulme, people always sat indoors in the evenings, doing their sewing or listening to the wireless; but here it was different. I walked past the houses, enjoying watching groups of people sitting on the verandas or on low walls, laughing and talking with each other. Some of them had brought their radios outside and they chattered away over the sound of the dance music, drinking Coca-Cola from the bottle. I noticed there wasn't a black person among them.

'I just think you could tell me where you're going, that's all.'

It was our third week in the Allendene and it was clear that things weren't going well for Freda.

'Just let me get on with my business, will you?' My father had his back turned away from Freda in their double bed. He was lying as far away from her as he could possibly get.

'And what am I meant to do while you're in the surgery with Gladys all day?' Freda almost spat her name.

'Look, we're all working bloody hard here to set up the sanctuary, so just shut up and give me a break, will you?'

My father and Alec had rented a room downtown in an office block. This they'd furnished as a surgery for the Triangle Band Healing Sanctuary, which they'd set up for a new Spiritualist circle they'd got in with in Johannesburg. The only trouble was that Freda had not been invited to join in. It was Gladys who had been kitted out in a smart new nurse's uniform. Freda was hopping mad about it. After all, she'd been promised by my father that she'd be the one sitting at his right hand and sharing in the glory once they'd set up the new sanctuary.

Freda wasn't letting up. 'And I suppose that little tart, Bunty, you keep going down the road to visit isn't my business either?'

I'm glad that I couldn't see my father's eyes when she said that. I didn't know how Freda dared tackle him head on. We both knew he could get really scary.

But he just called her a sour-faced cow and told her to shut up.

I knew, when they went to bed, that Freda was brewing for a fight. I'd seen her put on her pink nighty with ribbons earlier on, and when my Dad came to bed she'd tried as hard as she could to flirt with him. It was awful to listen to, especially as he was so cold and curt to her in response. When he saw the nighty he just said, 'You'll get cold. You'd better put a cardigan on.'

Another time, Freda had a bug and was throwing up into a bowl over the side of the bed. My father didn't ask her if she was okay, didn't even look up from his book. It was as if, now that he'd got to South Africa, he was going to try his hardest to show that he really didn't need Freda any more. He had other fish to fry, and one of them was obviously Bunty.

I'd tried then, as I tried now, to cut out the sound of their voices by lying with my good ear shoved as hard as it would go into my pillow.

Oh please will you just shut up. I can't stand it. I found myself furiously arguing with them in my head. I was feeling hot and sweaty by now and was longing to throw back my sheet and turn my pillow to its cooler side, but knew I didn't dare risk them hearing me move.

I felt like I'd been lying there for hours and was almost sobbing with frustration. *I've got to get some sleep. I've got school tomorrow. Will you just shut up!*

The next day, school was as bad as I feared. I'd been there a week now and Barnato Park Girl's School wasn't getting any better. Unlike my school in Hulme, this one was full of well-heeled, spotlessly dressed girls from the posh northern suburbs. With their Alice bands and their perfect cardigans around their perfect shoulders, they looked a very different breed to anything I knew. And, once they'd scented an outcast in their midst, they turned from me with a collective shudder.

Although I didn't have to play the part of a boy once we'd left the ship, my hair was still pretty short. That alone made it quite impossible for me to fit in with the young ladies of Barnato Park School. And my father soon saw to it that I would always be an outcast.

He had hit the roof when he saw the clothes' list. 'I don't bloody believe it! Three white piquet cotton dresses, if you please,' he snorted furiously. 'Six pairs white cotton ankle socks; two pairs black lace-up walking shoes with eight eye holes; one black blazer with brocade piping and school badge sewn on pocket; one white panama hat with school crest embroidered on hat band −'

At this he'd broken off, throwing the list down in disgust. 'Where am I going to get all this bleeding money from? Who do they think they are –?'

'Well, what do you expect me to do?' Freda asked, knowing that one way or another it would be her responsibility to sort me out.

'Get her a dress and a pair of shoes that'll last,' he said. 'And they can stuff the rest.'

When I'd gone into school in a less-than-white dress, a pair of shoes far too big for me, and an old pair of socks, I was hauled up in front of the class.

'Where's your blazer and hat?' the teacher, Mrs Poole, asked me.

'I don't have them,' I replied.

'Well, you'd better come with them tomorrow as there's a dress drill,' she said. 'Now, sit here at the front where I can see you and get out your arithmetic exercise book.'

'I don't have an exercise book,' I said quietly.

The other girls sniggered as Mrs Poole drew herself up indignantly. 'Were you not given a list of what you had to buy?' she asked. 'This is not England, you know.'

'My father's got the list.'

'You cannot come to class without your exercise books,' she said, closing the conversation.

Mrs Poole then reluctantly gave me a piece of paper to write on. All the other girls had pencil cases complete with set squares and protractors and all sorts of other unfamiliar items that had been on the list. I only had the pencil stub and ballpoint pen Dad had given me, along with one of his half-used jotter pads that he'd thrown in my face with a snort.

What the heck am I going to do now? I thought to myself. *I hardly dare ask him for this stuff, but even if I did he's never in.*

However, when I got home he was in and I did find the courage to confront him. I asked about the blazer. He went absolutely bonkers, swiping me across the face.

'Oh, you think the trees, the bloody trees are going to give me money?' he shouted. 'You'll just have to wait.'

And wait I did.

The next few days, it was the same routine – the dress drill and a ticking off by Mrs Poole – until finally she wrote a letter to my father. He moaned and complained the whole evening about it, finally throwing a couple of pound notes at Freda saying, 'Buy her a bloody blazer.'

So Freda took me to the shop at last and bought the blazer and hat on the dummy in the window as she didn't have enough money for one out of a box. The blazer had faded and the hat had a yellow tinge.

A week later, I was still feeling like a gawky sparrow in my grey socks. Only this time my name was being read out by the headmistress in assembly. I got up, blushing with shame, sensing several hundred smirking faces turned in my direction.

'Now girls, I want you to raise your hands if you can see what is wrong with Judith's appearance,' she said. 'We set a standard at Barnato Park which we expect every single girl to adhere to. It is just not good enough coming in looking like this.'

One prissy girl in the front immediately shot up her hand. 'Yes, Serena,' the head said, pointing at her.

'Well, miss, her dress looks all dirty round the hem and isn't ironed properly, and there's no school badge on the collar.'

'That's quite right. You must all have creases here and here on your dresses,' the head said, pinching the sleeves of my dress. She then made me kneel down. 'And you'll see that Judith's skirt is not the regulation length above the knee.'

'Anybody else?'

Another hand went up. 'She's meant to have white socks, turned down an inch,' another girl informed us. 'Hers aren't white, they're a sort of grey colour.'

One by one, every item of school clothing was criticized, until the most humiliating moment of all.

'And what's wrong with these?' The headmistress lifted my skirt so that the whole school could see my knickers, which weren't the regulation black.

I wanted to run away and never come back.

We got out of school at half past one and the heat on the streets was intense. We were forbidden to take our blazers off until we'd arrived home, which I thought was a stupid rule as by the time I got back to the Allendene I felt like a cooked chicken. I ran straight upstairs and peeled the white dress from my hot and sticky body.

I'd had to get into the routine of washing my dress every afternoon. It always had grass stains on it or muck from the wall we used to sit on at breaktime. I found it very tricky to get it clean as we only had a tiny basin in the corner of our room and the material of the dress seemed to suck up masses of water. It was almost impossible to wring out and there was water all over the floor by the time I'd finished. I had to borrow Freda's towel and roll my dress up in it in an attempt to soak it up.

Next, I took a coathanger and hung the dress at the open window to dry. I managed to borrow an iron from a lady downstairs which you had to plug into the electric light switch. It was pretty hopeless and didn't do the job of making the proper creases on the sleeves. I tried to get the dress flat but it never looked right – or quite clean.

Chapter Fifteen

*F*reda and my dad were getting on worse and worse. Their silences filled our room in the rare evenings they were both in and although neither of them hit me any more, they were often sniping at me. Once, I came into the room and found Freda sitting on the bed looking red eyed from crying. I suddenly felt a little bit sorry for her.

'Are you all right?' I asked her.

Freda didn't bother to look at me and I thought she wasn't going to reply. After a moment, though, she said, 'I wish I'd never come.'

I didn't know what to say to that, so I didn't respond. I was waiting for her to say that it was all my fault, that if I hadn't been in tow, she and Jack would be all right; but she didn't this time.

My dad refused to be brought down by Freda's mood. He continued to be in his element, filling the wardrobe with new suits and cravats, bought with some of the ill-gotten proceeds of the sanctuary as it turned out. It was as though here in South Africa he finally felt free to be the con man – a role that had always come naturally to him.

Freda wasn't the only one upset by my father's goings on. All his sharp suits and new girlfriends had to be paid for somehow. One evening, only a couple of months after we moved into the Allendene, we had a visit from Alec and Gladys.

Cathleen and I sat on the bed watching the row unfold. I felt a strange sense of relief that the Rippons had found out that my father wasn't to be trusted. I'd always liked Alec and it made me feel very uncomfortable that he was paying for our room at the Allendene and bankrolling the sanctuary. I had a horrible sense that it would only be a matter of time before my father and Freda had sucked him dry.

Alec was a mild-mannered, kindly man and I was quite amazed that he could be so feisty. He must have been really, really angry with my dad.

'I've had enough, Jack. Absolutely enough!' Alec was a small man but just now he almost looked tall. Gladys stood at his side, showing the quiet moral support she always gave her husband. I thought again what dignity she had.

My father didn't answer but wore a relaxed expression. Not quite insulting, but almost.

'We feel betrayed, quite frankly,' Alec went on. 'We've given our all to the sanctuary. Sold our house, for Christ's sake. Patients told us you were taking money out of the donation boxes. We didn't want to believe them, but Gladys saw you. You're a lousy fraudster, Jack.'

'What do you plan to do then?' my father said, clearly wanting to end the conversation but still sounding nonchalant.

'I've got my wife and child to consider,' said Alec. 'And there's no way we want anything to do with a con man like you. We're leaving before you can do any more damage. Quite frankly, you're very lucky I haven't called in the police.'

'Well, you'd better please yourself, then,' my dad said, moving over to the door and opening it.

Gladys took her cue, taking Cathleen with her, and walking out without a backward glance, dignified to the last. Alec looked suddenly deflated and very, very sad. Only a few weeks ago, he and dad had come up with a slogan for the sanctuary: 'New light, new hope, new truth'. Now his dreams of helping lost souls were in pieces. He didn't look at my father or Freda as he left the room.

I wonder what they're going to do now? I thought to myself. *Maybe they'll go back to England and buy their house back.*

But I had a feeling that they wouldn't give up quite yet; wouldn't want to go back to England so soon. That would be admitting they'd failed. We never saw the Rippons again.

Once they'd left the room, my father muttered, 'Good riddance to bad rubbish,' and I knew that he'd put them out of his mind just as soon as they'd walked out of the door. I'd never known him to feel a moment of remorse, or even embarrassment, and he wasn't going to start now. As far as he was concerned, that was the end of that particular gravy train for him. He'd go out looking for another tomorrow, no doubt.

I could tell that Freda was immediately in a much better mood. No more having to be the poor relation around Gladys; no more being left out in the cold while the other three played doctors and nurses at the Triangle Band Healing Sanctuary. I'm sure Freda thought that being on their own again would allow her to be my father's right-hand woman at last, standing with him on the platform at Spiritualist church events. After all, back in Hulme, that's what he'd always promised her.

'Don't worry, Jack,' she said to my father soothingly. 'We'll work out a plan. I'll get a job or something.'

My father didn't show much grace when she said that, but he didn't turn away from her.

Freda was true to her word and got a part-time job at a solicitor's firm called Schwartz, Fine and Kane as a filing clerk. My father happily took her money for the rent but showed no sign of wanting to be around her any more than before. In fact, if anything, they saw less of each other. Dad hardly came home at all, and soon Freda was staying out much more as well.

She'd made some friends at work who encouraged her to join the Italian Club, where she could play tennis and drink in the bar with other ex-pats. I noticed that Freda had started to look different too, wearing what she called her 'trews' – checked trousers that were very much in vogue then – instead of her usual frumpy skirts and dresses.

By now, she'd completely washed her hands of me. Apart from the odd gripe to my dad about how useless and sneaky I was, she ignored me completely. It was as if I wasn't there.

I was relieved not to be bullied as much by Freda any more, but I found myself feeling desperately lonely. There was no one I could talk to at school and instead of coming home to Gyp's enthusiastic welcome, as I would have done in Hulme, I'd get back to our empty boarding house with hours to kill before bedtime. I managed to while away some of the long hours of the afternoon and evening in the hotel lounge, picking out tunes on the piano; and a couple of times a week I would go to the library. I found that I had an unquenchable hunger for books about animals, particularly dogs. I read *Jock of the Bushveld* and *Old Yella* again and again. Reading them helped me grieve for Gyp, for I was still feeling the loss of her keenly.

My father was spending most of the time on the road, preaching to Spiritualist groups all over Witwatersrand. If I needed anything for school, like a book or a piece of sports kit, I knew I was done for. He was never around to ask.

One afternoon, on coming back to the hotel after school, I was shocked to find Dad in our room. I could tell he'd been waiting for me. He was holding a letter, crumpled in his fist. I guessed it must have been from the school and thought I'd be getting another 'money doesn't grow on trees' rant. I could almost feel my hair standing on end, hackles rising like a dog's, as I stood there.

'Who's the bloody traitor in the camp?' He spat the words at me.

I didn't say anything. Just waited. Steeling myself for a beating.

'How did your mother know you were here? You bloody wrote to her, didn't you?'

I shook my head. 'I didn't! I don't know how she found out.'

'Because of you, we've now got her damn solicitor sniffing around.' Dad flourished the letter furiously in my face. 'I don't know what he thinks he can do. But he's trying to make trouble. He's going to learn that possession's nine-tenths of the law. He, of all people, should know that. And she can go jump off a cliff for all I care. You're here with me, and that's an end of it.'

You've got me but you don't even want me! Why couldn't you just have left me behind with her? I don't understand! I thought as I stood there, listening to his ranting, watching the spittle fall on his beard.

Dad grabbed my arm and forced me to sit on his bed while he got a pen and piece of paper. Dictation time again. *I wonder what rubbish he'll make me write this time?*

'Sit there. Here, lean on this.' He put his briefcase on my knees. 'Write exactly what I say.'

My father forced me to write a letter to my mother's solicitor assuring him of my happiness. South Africa was a land of milk and honey, and I was having a wonderful time, apparently. Dad invented the most ridiculous, sickly-sweet fairytale. I couldn't believe for one moment that any educated, sensible person would believe a word of it.

'I have lots of friends and I love going down to the beach.'

We don't live anywhere near a beach!

'When I sit with my friends on our veranda we can see lots of sweet little monkeys in the trees.'

We live in the middle of a big city. Surely they won't fall for that?

I lay in bed that night thinking about my father. One question had always circled round and round my head: *Why does he keep me, when he finds me so repulsive to have around?* I knew that he needed Freda and me to act the part of his spotless family, giving him a perfectly respectable image. Without it, his congregation of blue-rinse ladies probably wouldn't trust him.

I always sensed, too, that my father wanted an easy target when he played his sadistic power games. The psychotic in him wanted me – and Freda too – under his control, so that he could twist the knife whenever and however he pleased, even if, for the most part, he couldn't be bothered.

I reckoned that Dad would have liked to have Mum under his control too, and it had never ceased to irk him that she'd broken free. Wanting to be locked in a perpetual battle with her, I supposed the best way he could do it was to use me as hostage.

Meanwhile, things at Barnato Park were going from bad to worse. I was the only immigrant child in the school and the teachers picked on me in class. Not one of them stopped to think I might need help and support. Every day I was met with the rigid disapproval of the whole miserable lot of them.

The other girls made me feel just as isolated. They came from homes where they were cosseted; where there were swimming pools and tennis parties. Where maids did all the fetching and carrying. They'd probably never even had to brush their own hair. There was always a servant around to do everything for them. All their lives, they'd been cushioned from the rest of the world, and from undesirables like me.

South Africa in the 1950s was indeed cut off from the rest of the world. The rules of apartheid had never been tougher or more rigid. On my first night in Berea, I'd wondered where all the black people were. Now I knew. They had to go back to their townships at night. After six in the evening, black people on the street who didn't have a special pass were arrested. I'd once seen two policemen dragging a black man along the street. Each had one of the man's legs over their shoulder so that he was hanging upside down, head bashing the pavement. The sheer brutality of the regime was clear, even to an eleven-year-old like me.

I'd seen signs everywhere in the city, telling black people which parks they could let their kids play in, which restaurants they could eat at, and which seats on the bus they could sit on. And I'd watched how people behaved.

How the park keeper would shoo away the black kids, pointing angrily at the notice on the gate: 'Whites Only. Europeans. No Blacks'. Or how a black person would step out into the road to make way for a white person, even if that person was a child. I was living in a place where even the pavement wasn't equally shared, and I didn't like it one bit.

The girls at my school were all clones, conditioned from an early age to think apartheid was normal. Fresh from England, I soon realized that I was the enemy. I wasn't ever going to be a part of the group. I hadn't inherited the moral superiority of the Afrikaner as my birthright.

One morning, in my Afrikaans class, I spoke up. I hadn't decided to challenge the status quo and if I'd thought about it beforehand I don't think I'd have dared. After all, as I saw it, I had eight hundred people against me at that school and no one fighting in my corner. But I'd had enough and I couldn't prevent myself blurting out. I'd seen intolerance and unfairness everywhere around me in South Africa, especially at Barnato Park.

Mrs Schmidt was our Afrikaans teacher. She was a middle-aged woman, dressed in an old-fashioned brown suit, pencil-thin, and as sour as a lemon. From the first day she had me in her class, she'd made it quite plain that she thought I had no business being there. In her eyes, I was scum — a British immigrant with none of the superior characteristics of her own master race of Afrikaners.

Mrs Schmidt didn't just teach us the Afrikaans language. She spouted about the superiority of the Afrikaner people like an ugly stone gargoyle. That morning, she was in full flood.

'You see, girls, God chose the Afrikaners to lead the country from darkness into light,' she explained. 'South

Africa needed our superior race – a white people with God on our side – to take the reins of leadership. That's what the Vortrekkers were fighting for.'

I felt the heat rising in me as she spoke. I looked around the room and saw the other girls all sitting dutifully straight-backed at their desks. *Do you really believe this rubbish?* I wanted to shout at them.

Once Mrs Schmidt had got into her stride, there was no stopping her. 'You see, the kaffirs, with their smaller and inferior brains – like monkeys' – needed a new race of leaders to lead the country,' she said. 'To give them the moral and spiritual education they were lacking before.'

I couldn't bear it any more. And besides, there was a question I just had to ask. So I stood up, scraping my chair back in a less than ladylike fashion. There was an audible, indrawn breath from the other girls.

'But, if the Africans are so bad,' I asked, 'why do the whites leave their kids to be looked after by them all day?'

It seemed like a perfectly sensible question to me. I'd seen the black nannies wheeling the white kids along in their prams in the park. There were never any white mums there. If that was so, then what Mrs Schmidt had just said didn't seem logical. I really did want to know the answer. I didn't get it though.

I thought Mrs Schmidt's eyes were going to pop clean out of her head. She looked as though I'd thrown acid in her face. As she stood there, speechless for a moment, I saw an ugly red flush spread upwards from her chest.

'Out!' Mrs Schmidt's scream was harsh. 'Out!'

Words had obviously failed her in her fury.

I stood outside the classroom waiting for the class to finish. As soon as I heard the bell that marked the end of the school day, I walked out of the building. Every step of the way home, I chewed over Mrs Schmidt's remarks until I was seething. I resolved then never, ever to set foot in her classroom again.

When I got back to the Allendene, I stomped into the lounge and flung myself down on the piano stool. *Bang, bang, plonkety-plonk*, I stabbed at the keys furiously. Life was so unfair.

At the end of the room, an old man was sitting. He was always there, never moving from his chair under the window. He'd told me his name was Mr Wolfe, but I'd hardly spoken to him before, except to ask him when I came in if it was all right if I played the piano. Occasionally, he'd ask me what tune I was trying to pick out. I loved Pat Boone's songs, especially *April Love* and Debbie Reynolds' *Tammy*. I'd sing the line first, *Tammy, Tammy, Tammy's in love*, then work it out on the keys. Mr Wolfe always nodded his old white head kindly and usually asked me to play it again.

This time, it must have been clear to the old man that I'd had a bad day. When I'd stopped plonking the keys for a moment, he cleared his throat.

'Are you all right, dear?' he asked kindly, in his ancient reed-like voice. 'Have you had a bad day at school?'

I nodded, my eyes suddenly filling up.

'Why don't you come over here and tell me about it?' Mr Wolfe patted the seat beside him.

I told him about Mrs Schmidt and what I'd said to her. He couldn't help smiling at that. But then he looked serious, gazing with his watery pale blue eyes into my own.

'There are many people like your Mrs Schmidt in the world,' he said. 'Do you see this number?' Mr Wolfe rolled up his sleeve to show me a faded blue number tattooed on the outside of his withered forearm.

I nodded. 'What's it for?'

'During the war, I was locked up by the Germans in a concentration camp,' he told me. 'And I saw some terrible things. Things I can still see and hear. And smell too. My family died, my friends died. And all because a group of people thought like your Mrs Schmidt.'

Mr Wolfe's shoulders slumped and he looked away. A few moments passed, and I thought he'd forgotten I was there. Then he turned to me again.

'The world hasn't changed,' he said.

I'm sure his words shouldn't have made me feel better, but somehow they did. It was good to know that at least one person understood, and that I had someone in my corner, after all.

Mr Wolfe struggled to his feet. When he was standing, I saw he was bent over, almost at a right angle to the ground. I thought it must have been odd to spend so much time looking at your shoes.

'Wait here a moment,' he said. 'I've got something for you.'

He walked over to a case next to the gramophone on the sideboard. He opened it and pulled out a record.

'I used to play this when I was upset,' Mr Wolfe told me, wiping the old '78 lovingly with his sleeve. 'It's the great Caruso, singing *Pagliacci*. It tells the story of a clown. A clown that laughed while his heart was broken.'

He carefully wound up the gramophone and lifted the arm to place the needle on the record. Then he stood there, as if lost in thought, while the wonderful tenor voice filled the shabby room. I was transported to another place, lit up by the music.

When it had finished, Mr Wolfe looked over to me with a smile. 'Feeling better now?' I nodded and smiled back.

'I'd like you to have my record,' he said to me.

Words failed me, but I gave my thanks to him silently. I knew he understood how much his gesture meant to me.

Only a couple of months after that Mr Wolfe died. One day he was in his chair by the window, and the next it was empty.

Chapter Sixteen

I was in the Hillbrow Library one afternoon when I noticed a poster on the noticeboard. None had ever caught my eye before, but I couldn't fail to notice this one. It was bright red and orange and had a big roaring lion painted on it with the words *Wilkies Circus*. Around the lion were little pictures of flying trapeze artists and a clown. I saw that the circus was opening the next weekend in the grounds just beyond the university.

I knew I had to be there. I'd always devoured every book on circuses I could find, here in the library and also back in Hulme. There was something about the life that really appealed to me. Enid Blyton's *The Circus of Adventure* was a particular favourite. The performers and stage hands seemed like one big family, and yet they weren't a family in the real sense at all. I knew that many of them came from distant corners of the globe, and that some of them were probably runaways. And the idea of runaways had always, unsurprisingly, had its appeal.

I loved gymnastics and had always dreamed of swinging from the trapeze, or doing stunts on the back of a palomino pony. In our room in the Allendene, I used to practise doing the splits or walking on my knees in the lotus position; and outside in the courtyard, I'd do hand-stands up against the wall. Gym was the only thing I excelled at at school, and my teacher said I must be double-jointed. I was often asked to demonstrate to the other girls how to do a somersault from the wooden horse or backflips on the beam. There were lots of things I couldn't master though, and I was longing to see how the circus performers managed to get it right.

It was quite a way to the circus grounds. I had to walk through Hillbrow and Braamfontein, and past the jail and the university. I could see the flags on the big top long before I got there, waving cheerily against the cloudless blue sky. When I climbed up a grassy embankment to the fenced-off area there it was – a big cream coloured tent, with red and white striped sides.

I didn't go in the main entrance but climbed over the fence at the side. I could see families queuing at the ticket office. Some of them were already milling around the cara-vans and trucks, killing time before the show began. No one seemed to mind them being there.

I could hear snorting and whinnying coming from a big, long tent and went straight to it. Inside were the horses and cream ponies, llamas and camels, each in its own stall. The horses had beautifully plaited manes and tails, just as I'd imagined they would. At the end of the tent were two elephants, tethered by the foot, who lifted their trunks when they saw me.

I stayed a few minutes in the animal tent, soaking it all up, before moving on. Outside, I could see a group of kids gathered at the front of an open-sided trailer and eating candyfloss. When I got closer, I saw two tigers inside, pac-ing back and forth behind the bars. I went and stood behind the rail in front which had a sign which read,

'Please don't feed the animals'. I supposed that if there hadn't been a sign there, some of the kids might have been stupid enough to give them candyfloss.

I made my way around the side of the big top to the back, carefully avoiding tripping over the guy ropes and wooden pegs. There I found a place where the canvas had been pinned back to reveal a large, corridor-like backstage area. I went in. All the props were laid out ready for the show, including a miniature red open-topped car, a couple of unicycles, and a see-saw. Hanging from hooks on the white canvas was a row of plumed headdresses for the horses. Everything looked so ship-shape and orderly.

I wasn't on my own for more than a couple of minutes. The first people to come along were two African circus hands, rolling the big yellow tubs which I guessed that the elephants would stand on. I moved quickly aside, flattening myself against the canvas, so that I wouldn't get in the way. A moment later, two men with shiny black hair walked past me from the direction of the ring. They were wearing dressing gowns, open at the front, and underneath I could see they were wearing tight silver trousers. No one stopped to ask me what I was doing there. They didn't seem to care, and I could sense that their minds were wholly intent on the job in hand.

A group of musicians walked past me, climbed a ladder to a platform above the ring, and started tuning up. When I heard the cymbals and trombones, I felt my whole body wake up, as if charged by volts of electricity. I wasn't the only one to feel thrilled by the music. Inside the big top, I could hear the excited buzz from the audience, and the sound of the last stragglers rushing to take their seats. Even the animals seemed to feel the excitement.

A few minutes before the show began, a pair of circus hands carried an arched cage into the backstage area and set it down. Moments later, the big cats were sent down a tunnel into it, ready for the first act.

What followed was a noisy kaleidoscope of colour, sound, and movement as one act after another came on and off stage, seamlessly, like a regiment of the best-trained soldiers you could ever imagine. Every prop, I realized, had been lined up the right order to be used so there was no fussing or noise. I saw the lions and their tamer — a strong-looking, rather dour man; a family of chimps — the girls in little frilly skirts and the boys in shorts and dickie bows; the clowns with their tiny red car; and a little girl who rode on the back of a pony in her tutu. She couldn't have been much older than seven.

All the while, the band played great oomp-pah-pah waltzes and the artists and animals skipped and paced, alert to their cues. As I stood there enthralled by the whole, wonderful spectacle I knew I was utterly hooked.

There was nothing going on at home to deter me from spending every spare moment of the next few days at the circus. I bunked off school each morning, and the longer I spent there the more I realized I couldn't go back to how things were before — the daily misery of school, and my loneliness in the long afternoons and evenings; and, on the very few occasions my dad and Freda had both been in, the poisonous silence between them.

My father had a way of looking straight through Freda as if she wasn't there. I knew that stare only too well and it still managed to terrify me. It made you feel like you were no better than a worm, and Freda was obviously hurt that Dad used it on her. She rarely asked for anything of him, though – her pride wouldn't let her – and she never broke down in front of us. But I knew that when she used to leave the room to let off steam, she'd invariably go out for a walk and a cry as her eyes would look red and swollen later on. Freda was a tough one, though, and I knew she'd rather die than let my dad see she was hurt.

As the week went on, the circus folk got used to my hanging about the place. There were plenty of poor white kids in Braamfontein, where the rows of cement semi-detached bungalows were the nearest thing to a white slum Johannesburg had. I'm sure everyone just presumed I was from there.

As I became bolder, I started to explore more. My favourite thing was stroking the animals in their stalls. I learned to leave the llamas alone, though, as they used to spit at your eyes without warning. Crack shots, they were.

The only place I hadn't dared venture inside was the big top, but I studied the outside of it and saw how it was put up; how the guy ropes were stretched down to the big pegs and tightened. The caravans and red-and-yellow trucks parked in a circle around it were mostly used for storage. The circus families, I discovered, stayed in their own steam train parked in a railway siding across the field.

One day, I was in the animal tent stroking the ponies when a boy came in carrying a bucket of feed. He was blond and athletic-looking and looked a couple of years younger than me. I didn't know his name then, but I knew who he was as I'd seen him with his dad, the lion tamer.

The boy smiled at me and started emptying oats into the horses' troughs. I took a few steps towards him.

'What's the name of this one?' I asked, stroking the nose of one of the palomino ponies.

'That's Lady,' the boy said.

'She's my favourite,' I said. A few moments later, I added, 'What's your name, then?'

'Carl. What's yours?'

'Judy.'

And there it was.

After that, I hung around with Carl quite a bit. He was a gentle boy who didn't think it strange spending time with a girl and I felt immediately comfortable with him. Tall and graceful, he had inherited his Dad's quiet confidence and had a wonderful way with all the animals. I watched him wash the elephants or screw the horses' plumes into their harnesses before the show. Once, I helped him catch the llamas in the paddock. Carl said they always gave him the runaround and he looked grateful when I managed to grab them pretty quickly, ducking and dodging out of the way of their perfectly aimed bullets of spit.

On the Wednesday, as I watched the artists running back on stage at the end of the show to take their bows, I heard the roaring and clapping from the audience and watched the sheer joy in the faces of the performers. I could see that the animals got a huge kick out of the applause too, and I watched the chimps hanging around the necks of Billy and Marion Dash as they came out of the ring, giving them big, sucking kisses on their cheeks. For a moment it was as if the scene stopped still, as if crystallized in front of me. And the thought came to me then with such clarity – *I've got to be part of this.*

People were happy at Wilkies. I never saw anyone carping or criticizing, like Dad and Freda. I asked myself, *How can a family this big manage to get along so well, organizing everything so it runs like clockwork? Freda and Dad can't even manage to rub along together for one minute without going for each other's throats – or, more often, mine.*

Still feeling the glow of my day at the circus, I returned at five o'clock to the Allendene. I wasn't expecting to see Freda or my dad there, but they were in when I got back and I could tell a nasty row was brewing. Later that evening, I lay in bed with my head turned to the wall, my good ear pressed hard into the pillow. It wasn't any use, though. I could still hear every word.

'You're never at home.'

'Well, you're never in either.'

'I know you've got someone else. You don't even bother to cover your tracks. It's always Cherie this, and Cherie that. I'm not stupid, you know.'

'God! Lay off, will you.' Dad spat back at Freda. 'You'd drive anyone away with your carping and complaining.'

'You only brought me to South Africa so that you had someone to take care of your brat.' I could almost feel Freda's malevolent, slitted eyes on me when she said that.

And there it always ends, I thought. *With me. The brat. All my life I've felt that it would be better if I wasn't here. If I just disappeared. Well, I'll show you both. I'm old enough now. This time, I'm going to do it. I'm going to disappear for good.*

The thoughts pounded round my head and, as the minutes passed, the more I became convinced of my own logic. They didn't want me here. I didn't want to be here. And what I wanted, more than anything in my whole life, was to be at the circus. There was the answer.

I felt suddenly as hard as steel. *This isn't a game, Judy,* I said to myself. *If I'm really going to run away, then I'll need to get every tiny detail right. Cover my tracks. Because, if he catches me, God only knows what he'll do.*

I always knew that my dad had in him the power to kill me. He just needed the excuse.

Eventually, that night, my dad and Freda stopped rowing and went to sleep, their backs turned away from each other in a rigid stalemate. In the quiet of the night hours, I planned my escape, and when it was all sorted in my mind I finally felt able to relax and fell into a sound sleep.

The next morning, I went down to breakfast earlier than usual, dressed for school. I knew it was important that Sunday, the head waiter, saw me in my uniform when he handed me my packed lunch. Chances were that Freda and my dad would both be out for a few nights following their row, and so long as no one reported anything out of the ordinary to them this morning, it could be days before either of them would know I was missing.

I went and hid in the alcove under the stairs. From there I could keep tabs on people's comings and goings. First, I heard Freda coming down to breakfast, then leaving for work. Then I heard my dad's footsteps on the stairs about twenty minutes later.

As soon as my father had walked into the dining room, I ran up the stairs to our room. My plan was to hide in the wardrobe until I knew for certain that he'd left for the day. It was the only space big enough for me. I opened the door and quickly decided that it would be too dangerous to hide on the side my dad hung his suits, in case he went to get something and saw me standing there. Instead, I crouched in a squat on a shelf on the other side, where my dad kept his socks. On the inside of the wardrobe door was a rack for his ties and cravats. I looped one of them over the bar so that I could close the door behind me, leaving a tiny crack so that I could see what was going on in the room.

Only once did I let myself wonder what Dad would do if he found me crouching behind his shirts, but then I quickly dispelled the thought. I was frightened enough already. *My legs are getting sore,* I thought to myself, after ten minutes had gone by. *What if I sneeze? What if the shelf gives way and I fall?*

Then I heard my dad's footsteps in the corridor outside. The door swung open and he came into the room. At one point, he moved so close to the wardrobe that I could hear him breathing and smell his aftershave through the crack in the door. I was certain that he must have heard the hammering of my heart. It seem deafening to me.

Oh God! I've got cramp in my knees. I'm going to fall!

I hung on there, desperately, willing my dad to leave, but he seemed to take an age fiddling about in his briefcase and folding his newspaper. Finally, he took his jacket off the back of the chair and put it on. *Please go. Just go!*

At last, I heard him close the door. I stayed in the wardrobe long after I heard him go down the stairs, mentally counting his footsteps, calculating where he must have reached. *He'll have left the building. He'll be walking past the cars. Down the street. At the tram stop . . .*

I couldn't wait any longer. I knew the cleaning girl would shortly let herself in to make the beds. I got out of the wardrobe, my legs so cramped that they almost buckled under me, and quickly packed my brown school case with my shorts and shirt. It was going to be a real bore having to lug my school books around in it but I couldn't leave them in the room.

I was nervous having to walk the same route that my father's tram took, but I reckoned he'd be ten minutes or so ahead of me. I walked fast, feeling anxious the whole way. When I reached the circus grounds, half an hour later, my school dress was already soaked in sweat, although it was still early. And even then, I couldn't relax until I knew that I'd managed to hide my case.

I planned to sleep in a horse box I'd found. There didn't seem to be much stored in it, other than a few blankets and bridles. I was early enough to be able to let myself in without being seen as the artists and their families hadn't yet left their apartments on the train. I managed to steer clear of a couple of hands who were going about their business, mucking out and feeding the animals.

After checking the coast was clear, I walked quickly up to the horse box and climbed inside. I quickly changed out of my dress and put on my shorts and shirt, hiding my case under a blanket. Once I'd got changed out of my school clothes, I felt such a sense of liberation. I'd been having to wear my uniform, on the weekdays at the circus, and it was only now that I felt I'd truly escaped.

That day, instead of having to leave after the afternoon show, I was able to stay and watch the evening one as well. It felt wonderful not having to drag myself back to the Allendene. I hid behind one of the caravans and watched the dusk slowly darken the sky over the circus ground, waiting while the tired performers finished putting away their props before going home to their train. When all was quiet, I slipped out of my hiding place and crept like a shadow along the side of the animal tent, edging my way towards the horse box. I had to tread carefully as there were guy ropes everywhere, waiting to trip the unwary.

Just as I was about to make my way across to the horse box, I froze. I could hear the sound of whistling. Then someone's footsteps, making their way towards the animal tent. A moment later, I recognized Mr Wilkie, the circus owner, rounding the side of the tent, holding a torch. *He must have seen me! He must have!*

I held my breath and flattened myself against the canvas. He walked past, not more than five yards from me, and disappeared inside the tent to check on the animals. I could hear his voice, talking tenderly to the horses, and could imagine them gently huffing back at him through their big, round nostrils.

A couple of minutes later, Mr Wilkie left and I felt able to breathe again. I waited until I was absolutely sure the coast was clear, then moved out of the shelter of the animal tent and made my way to the horse box. Once I'd quietly let myself in and closed the back it was completely dark inside, but I managed to find my school case and open it. Inside was the sandwich Sunday had given me for my packed lunch that morning. I tucked into it hungrily, reflecting for a moment what an age it seemed since I'd left the Allendene. A whole world away from me now.

I lay down in the dusty darkness with a blanket around me. It stank strongly of horse, but I soon got used to the smell. *I'd better find somewhere to wash tomorrow*, I thought to myself. *I'm really going to stink*. My mind sleepily started to move through my plans for the next day, but it wasn't long before I was asleep. I slept very soundly, never hearing the sounds of the animals stirring in their tent next to me. It had been a long day. I'd been awake half of the night before working out my escape, and now I'd really done it.

I'd planned to be up and out the next morning before anyone was about but hadn't realized quite how early the circus day started. Usually, I'd rely on the dawn light waking me, but it was dark inside the horsebox so I'd slept through. The next thing I knew, the back was flung open and the light streamed in, waking me with a start.

I sat up confused, not immediately knowing where I was, and found myself face to face with Carl, who looked just as shocked as I was.

'What are you doing here?'

I didn't say anything for a moment, just stared at him wide-eyed. But I knew I'd have to say something to keep him there and stop him going to tell his dad. I'd never opened up about my troubles to anyone before, but something told me that it would be the right time to do so now. I didn't have to tell him everything, just a little to get him on side.

'Please don't tell anyone,' I begged Carl. 'I couldn't go back home. I've run away.'

'Why?' the boy asked. 'What are your mum and dad going to say when you don't come back?'

'My mum's in England,' I told him. 'And my dad's always hitting me. Most of the time I'm left on my own.'

Carl stood a moment, thinking. Finally, when he spoke, I knew I had him on my side.

'Well, it won't be safe staying here. People come in and out to fetch horse blankets. They'll find your case.'

'But where can I go?' *He'll think of somewhere. Then I'll be be able to stay.*

'I know just the place,' Carl replied. He was starting to enjoy himself now. 'At the back of the train there's a carriage that's used for storing props. No one ever goes in there, so you'll be quite safe.'

'Shall we go now?' I asked

'No, there'll be people about having breakfast and stuff. We'll go later when they're all busy here. Just hide your case for now.'

The rest of the morning, Carl took me under his wing and I followed him about while he did his chores.

I grabbed the chance to wash whilst spraying the elephants with the hose. *I'll be able to have my bath with them every day*, I thought to myself, happily.

Later on, when there was a lull and we wouldn't be missed, Carl led the way across the field to the circus train. 'I'll take you through it from the front,' he said. 'Then you can see where everybody lives.'

We passed through the train, along a corridor which ran alongside the compartments. I was enthralled by what I saw. Each had been fitted out like a proper room in miniature. There were rugs on the floors and frilly curtains at the windows. Cheerful pictures hung on the walls, and some of the rooms had bookcases. Everything was so neat and cosy.

Towards the back of the train was the most extraordinary carriage of all. I stared at the rooms in amazement. Carl told me that they belonged to Marion and Billy Dash. He grinned as I stood there, gawping.

'They don't have kids of their own,' Carl whispered to me. 'So the chimps have their own room and everything.'

The chimps' bedroom was a wonderful sight, like something out of Goldilocks and the Three Bears. Each chimp had his own little bed, complete with cuddly toys, and on a floor in a neat row were their potties. I realized that the Dashes probably loved the chimps just as much as they would their own kids.

I hope I'll get a chance to help look after them, I thought to myself. I'd been longing to feel their skinny arms clinging around my neck as I'd seen them do with Marion and Billy. Their arms were so long that they looked like they'd be able to wind round more than once.

At the end of the train, Carl opened the door of the box room. 'Nobody ever comes in here.'

I looked around me and saw piles of old costumes, shoes and boxes. We pushed some of them aside and made enough space for me to lie down.

'Here, these'll do for a bed.' Carl handed me a rug and some pieces of fur, which I unfolded and laid flat. I then rolled up some bits of material to make a pillow.

Carl stood with his hands on his hips, satisfied I'd be okay now. 'Come on, hide your case, and let's go.'

'Wait,' I said. 'Let me just move these,' I pulled two boxes either side of the bed we'd made, then laid an old cloak over the top of them, making a kind of tent. Now if anyone came in, they wouldn't be able to see me.

'Here, it's best to leave this way,' Carl said, leading me out of the back of the train onto a little platform and down some steps. 'It's great your room's at the back. You'll be able to come and go without anyone seeing.'

When we got back to the grounds, Carl told his dad I was new at the circus and that I was his friend. Mr Fischer, the lion tamer, was a man of few words and didn't say much, but he agreed that I could help Carl feed the animals.

As luck would have it, I also got to help grooming and dressing the horses. The circus hand who usually helped look after them hadn't turned up that morning and Harry Carry, their trainer, was looking fractious when we saw him.

'Carl, I'm going to need your help,' he grumbled. 'I'm never going to have them ready for the show at this rate. Your friend can help too if she wants.' Harry was looking at me and, although he was obviously feeling hassled, I saw a kindly twinkle in his eyes. 'I've seen how gently you handle them, so I reckon they'll be in good hands if you want the job.'

I nodded vigorously and found myself standing straight as a pole. *Yes, sir!*

'Just help Carl muck them out and feed them first thing. Then you'll need to get them to the paddock. And before the afternoon show, there's the grooming and dressing to be done.' Harry gave his instructions, then looked at his watch. 'Right, we haven't got long before the show, so you two had better get cracking.'

Carl gave me the plaiting of the manes and tails to do. 'That's more of a girl's job. You'll be better at it than me,' he said.

When I'd finished on the first horse, I asked him if what I'd done was okay. He came over and had a look.

'They're too fat,' Carl said, looking at my sausage-shaped plaits. 'Here, you need to part the mane like this.' He divided the hair in half and showed me how to plait an extra row underneath.

I got it right the next time and soon started making good headway. Carl was right. I was more nimble-fingered than him.

When we'd finished with the horses, Carl took me round to see the lions and tigers. I could tell he felt really proud of them. He stood squarely and spoke to them in a deeper voice than usual when he put his hand through the bars and ruffled the fur behind one of the tiger's ears.

'My dad says you've got to let them know who's master,' he said. 'They can sense if you're afraid.'

I didn't feel afraid of the tigers at all, although I didn't feel sure enough of my ground to follow Carl's lead.

'First you need to let the animals get used to you. Make friends with them.'

I thought of Carl's dad and how, when I'd watched him practising for the show, he'd put his head into the mouth of the lion. You surely wouldn't want to be anything *but* friends if you had to pull a stunt like that day in day out.

'But why does your dad use the whip if he wants to keep them on his side?' I asked Carl.

'He doesn't touch them with it,' Carl explained. 'Watch him tomorrow at rehearsal. He just uses the whip to get their attention and tell them when to move.'

We walked over to the lions' cage. There were three of them lying there, dozing in the sun. When they saw Carl, the two lionesses half opened their eyes sleepily, then closed them again, but the lion got up and padded over to him.

'You soppy old thing,' Carl said to him, then turned to me. 'I bet you didn't think he was such an old softy when you heard Dad making him give that big roar, did you?'

I'd heard the lion roaring in the show and the audible quiver of terror that ran through the kids in the audience. *I bet they wouldn't believe it if they saw him now*, I thought as I watched his old toothless mouth positively dribbling with pleasure as Carl stroked him under the chin.

'I love it when he and Dad lie on the ground and pretend to be in bed together. You'll see it tomorrow,' Carl laughed. 'This one puts his paw over Dad's shoulder. It's really funny.'

After my first proper introduction to the lions and tigers I went to see them every day, taking Carl's advice – *First you need to let the animals get used to you.* I would stand by their cage so they'd get used to my smell, and then inch my way forward, little by little, each day. Eventually, I put my hand through the bars of the tiger's cage and tickled behind Suki's ears. Just like any ordinary cat, she loved it, and rubbed against my hand.

I'd always felt I could trust animals; be myself with them. Understandably, I was wary around my own kind.

However, something momentous was happening to me at the circus. It was as if the sun had come out after a bleak rainy season and I felt myself unfurling like a flower, opening myself to the whole experience. I was no longer feeling like a piece of jigsaw in the wrong box. Here I fitted in and could be myself at last.

Chapter Seventeen

arl told me I'd need to meet him earlier than usual the next morning as Friday was rehearsal day. Instead of needing to get the animals ready in time for the afternoon show, they had to be fed and exercised first thing.

I slept well in my train compartment. I didn't need a blanket, as the fur we'd laid out as a mattress was very warm. As soon as it was light, I got up and set off across the field to the circus ground, where Carl had arranged to meet me.

When I got there, a couple of hands were already going about their business. As I sat on the grass waiting for Carl, I thought how confident they seemed compared to the other black people I'd seen on the streets of Johannesburg. Even Sunday, our head waiter at the Allendene, who was always efficiently businesslike in his white suit and red fez, wasn't treated half as well as the hands at Wilkies Circus.

Everybody at the circus had a job to do, for the good of the whole, and there wasn't an obvious hierarchy. Even Mr Wilkie, who owned the circus, never lorded it over anyone. He just expected everyone – people and animals – to work hard to create the best possible show and to make the audience happy. It was as simple as that. And I'd watched with awe at how every little cog in the machine moved with well-greased perfection.

When Carl arrived, rubbing sleep out of his eyes and looking tousled in his leather trousers and braces, he took me first to wash the elephants. Mary and her baby, Lily, were tethered by the ankle near to a tap. When we uncoiled the hose and turned the water on, they both trumpeted with excitement.

'Try lifting up your arm like this,' Carl swung his arm up in the air, vertical in front of his face. 'Watch!'

Both animals knew their cue and lifted their trunks in the air, mimicking him. I giggled and tried it too. Both elephants opened their mouths when they raised their trunks and made adorable little noises that sounded a bit like yawns.

'They like being tickled on their tongues too,' said Carl. 'Try it.'

I moved forward and reached out to Lily. Her tongue was a pinky-grey colour and there was dribble hanging down from the sides of her mouth. I scratched it with my fingertips, which she seemed to like.

By now I was soaking wet and took the opportunity to rub myself down. Taking a shower with my clothes on was surprisingly effective and it didn't take long for them to dry in the sun. I knew that, without a comb, my hair had become a tangled bush, but I didn't mind, and knew no one else would either. That was the joy of the circus; no one judged you by what you wore or what you looked like. And there were no more horrid school assemblies and dress drills for me now. Every time I thought of what I was missing I wanted to whoop with joy.

As we walked to the animal tent with our buckets of feed, Mr Wilkie came up to us. He was a stocky man in his fifties with the kindest twinkle in his eyes.

'Everything okay, kids?' he asked.

'Yes, thanks, Uncle Whilma.' Carl always called Mr Wilkie by this name.

Mr Wilkie turned to me. 'You're new here, aren't you?' he asked. 'Harry says you're getting on well with the horses.'

I smiled shyly, but really pleased by the compliment. 'It's great,' I said.

'Any good worker is welcome at my circus,' Mr Wilkie said. 'And do feel free to watch the rehearsal today. It's the only way to learn.'

It was wonderful having him say that. Carl had told me that the kids usually watched rehearsals, but it was good to know that I'd been given special permission by Mr Wilkie himself.

And I want to learn, I thought to myself. *I'll watch how they do it today and practise and practise until I get it right.*

I sat with Carl and a couple of the other kids in the big top. In the ring, the ringmaster called the artists in, group by group to rehearse. It was all very orderly as the performers knew only too well that one slip might mean injury.

The first on were the clowns. One of them was a dwarf. His companion was as tall and thin as a beanpole. They looked very funny together.

Carl whispered in my ear. 'The little one's Dickie,' he said. 'I expect you've heard of him. He's really famous.'

'What's the other one called?' I asked.

'Pickie,' he answered. 'There are two other clowns as well, Charlie – who does the Charlie Chaplin act – and Alan, the miserable Pierrot.'

I'd seen the clown with tears painted on his face. 'He's not really miserable, is he?'

'Not for real. He's a laugh.'

We stopped whispering to watch Dickie and Pickie. The little clown was sitting in the red Noddy car I'd seen backstage on my first day and was driving it around the ring. He looked so funny, waving and smiling at the empty rows of seats and I wondered what was going to happen next. Pickie stepped out in his big shoes at that moment and must have pulled a lever or something because the next thing, Dickie's seat had flipped him right up in the air. The little clown was extraordinarily agile and managed to hit the ground, roll into a somersault, and get back on his feet in an instant. I laughed and laughed.

The two clowns practised their next knock-about act over and over again. Dickie, I could see, was an exacting sort of task-master and wouldn't give up until their timing was absolutely perfect. I saw what strenuous work it was, although in the show it must have looked effortless. Dickie's acrobatic talent really was extraordinary. He tripped and somersaulted and could flip, as if on springs, several feet in the air. Pickie was wearing an enormous pair of shoes that extended way past his toes. They were so long that Dickie kept tripping over them. I was in stitches. *No wonder you're such a famous clown,* I thought.

All through the morning the acts came on one by one. Sometimes, one of the kids would be called over to join in and practise a stunt with their dad.

'They're allowed a little slot of their own in the actual show,' Carl told me. 'It's good practice for them and the audience loves to see the little ones try something out.'

I was impressed by how the families treated the kids. Each was learning something and every time they did it right, they'd be heaped with praise. I watched one girl doing ballet on a horse's back and a boy juggling.

Even the tiniest child would have a go at learning how to somersault.

As I watched Susie Wilkie, who couldn't have been more than three or four, doing a handstand on one of the acrobat's hands, I felt almost wistful for a moment. *They're given so much encouragement. Look at them being clapped and patted on the back. No one ever says, 'You didn't do that right, you stupid kid.'*

At noon, everyone stopped for lunch. The other kids all went back to the train with their families, but Carl took me along to where the hands were being given hotdogs and chips. The lady who was frying our sausages was the same stallholder who sold food to the audience in the interval. The previous day, she'd also given us breakfast, but as this was rehearsal day we'd gone without that morning. Now Carl and I were so hungry we didn't say a word to each other as we wolfed the food down.

Afterwards, we sat on the grass in the sun. I was full of questions, and Carl didn't seem to mind my firing them at him almost continuously.

The first thing I wanted to know was when we were moving on. The question had been nudging at the back of my mind. I knew I wouldn't feel safe until we'd left Johannesburg.

'We've got another couple of weeks here,' Carl said. 'And then we're going to the grounds near Zoo Lake.'

My heart sank. *Only as far as Zoo Lake?* It couldn't have been much worse. Zoo Lake was in the northern suburbs. *And the northern suburbs is where most of the girls in my class live,* I thought to myself, with a distinct feeling of unease.

I filed the thought away in the back of my mind for the moment, but over the next weeks it would frequently surface; and when it did, my stomach always gave a sickening lurch. I reckoned that my dad probably hadn't found out yet that I'd gone but at some point soon he'd know I was missing.

Maybe he won't care, I told myself hopefully. *Perhaps he'll just be glad to get shot of me. When we get to Zoo Lake, he probably won't be bothered to come all that way to fetch me, even if he did find out I was there.*

The rest of the afternoon was just as good as the morning. The chimps were on next and came into the ring chattering with excitement. Billy carried in their little table and chairs, and four of the chimps sat down to tea while one of them pretended to fill their cups from a teapot. Many years later, chimps that Marion and Billy had trained were used for the famous PG Tips advertisements.

I turned to Carl. 'Do you think Marion would ever let me help get them ready for the show?' I asked.

'I don't see why not,' he replied. 'You're really good with the animals. I heard Harry Carry talking to my dad about it.'

I flushed with pride and resolved to ask Marion soon.

A moment later, Carl got up. 'I'd better be off,' he said. 'To do the nastiest job of the day. You're jolly lucky you don't have to be on poo duty.'

I knew what Carl was referring to, and I agreed with him – it *was* the nastiest job of all. Even nastier than having a llama spit in your eye. I'd seen Carl do it before and I didn't envy him one bit.

Before the horses came into the ring, he would have to stick his bare hand up their bottoms and scoop out the poo. Otherwise, he explained to me, 'they make their messes all over the ring and it's a bit of a disaster'.

'What about the other animals?' I asked him.

'Well, my dad does the elephants,' he said, with a grin. 'And the llamas and camels get away without having it done. They just do little beads, so it's not so bad.'

I couldn't help grimacing, thinking of what it must feel like to have your bare hand in all that smelly poo. Still, I supposed you got used to it.

In a break before the next act, I thought about Carl and how friendly he'd been to me. I reckoned he probably didn't have anyone his own age to hang out with. All the other circus kids were quite a bit younger than him and he didn't have any brothers or sisters. He didn't have a mum either – it was just him and his dad.

When I'd asked him about school he'd told me that he was going to boarding school the following year.

'All the circus kids go when they're old enough,' he said. 'Then leave when they're fifteen.'

'Aren't you scared of going?' I asked him.

'It'll be okay, I expect,' he said. 'I'll get to come back in the holidays and train with my dad.'

I'd seen the younger kids sitting at a table in the field with a woman I'd guessed was their teacher. Mr Wilkie must have had to hire her so the little ones could keep up with their reading and sums.

I reckon I could put up with school if it was like that, I thought. *Sitting in the field in the sun in my shorts.* A very different kettle of fish from snooty old Barnato Park.

On another occasion I'd asked Carl what he did when the circus packed up for the winter.

'We go to the farm, our winter quarters,' he told me. 'It's only a few weeks before the tour starts again and there's masses to do. They've got to invent all the new acts.'

I hadn't wondered before how the artists had time to

come up with their acts. I'd simply imagined they had the odd new idea and tacked it on as they went.

'I suppose the audience would get bored if they see the same act next year when they come to Wilkies,' I said.

'They sure would,' agreed Carl. 'And anyway, the artists really need a change by the end of the season. You should see them at the start of the new one; they get really nervous and make quite a lot of mistakes in the first few shows.'

Mistakes, I realized, weren't viewed here as something dreadful that had to be punished. This came as a revelation to me. Mistakes, in fact, were a necessary part of getting things right, Harry Carry had explained.

'You just get back on the horse. And even if you do something wrong in front of the audience, you make them wait while you try it again. And again, if needs be. Otherwise, you'll get spooked, and nerves can be ruinous for a circus performer.'

The rest of the afternoon went by in a whirl. The last of the acts to come on were the trapeze artists. Five Italians – all one family – took it in turns to climb the rope ladder to a little platform forty feet above the ring. I noticed, before trying a stunt, that they each checked their own gear, and each other's, very carefully.

'You don't want to find yourself spinning in the air by a wrist strap that's not been properly checked,' said Carl with a shudder.

Before they took hold of the bar, I saw the performers rubbing some sort of powder on their hands and forearms.

'It's rosin, to stop the sweat making them slip,' Carl explained. 'And they have to wear bandages on their wrists to help the other person hang on as well.'

I'd always imagined that trapeze artists grabbed each

other by the hands, but when I watched them now I saw that they always went for each other's wrists.

The flying trapeze was a magical act to watch. As I sat there, entranced, I wondered how they'd ever got the timing right. Once one artist had left his swing to perform a triple somersault, how on earth did the other one work out exactly where he had to be to catch hold of the first one's ankles? It simply boggled my mind. *You're falling through the air and you can't even see the other person!*

'They do get it wrong loads of times in rehearsal,' said Carl. 'That's how they get it right in the end.'

And indeed, moments later, one of the performers missed his timing and tumbled through the air into the net below. He looked really irritated as it meant he had to go through the palaver of climbing all the way up again.

One of the family was a girl of about my age who walked across a tightrope in a tutu. I'd seen her practising her ballet positions with the ballet mistress earlier on and had watched her very carefully, knowing I'd want to try the same moves later that evening in my railway carriage.

Now the girl was standing on one leg, wobbling slightly, twenty feet above the ring. I watched her with awe, and not a little envy.

'She's in a harness today, as it's rehearsal,' said Carl. 'But in the show she has to do it without.'

Her dad was walking below her, mirroring her steps, and at the ready in case she fell. 'Is he allowed to follow her like that in the real thing?' I asked Carl.

'Yes. They always have to have someone there to catch them,' he replied. 'It's a rule at Wilkies.' Then he got up and tapped my arm. 'Come on, lazy, we'd better go and feed the animals.'

The rehearsal had awakened a whole new enthusiasm in me for the circus. From that day on, I spent every spare minute practising my backflips. Something I found particularly difficult was trying to come out of a crab into an elegant handstand, legs neatly together. However much I tried, I couldn't quite manage it.

One afternoon, a couple of days later, Dickie came up to me while I was trying to balance a broomstick handle on my chin. When I saw him, I let it drop.

'You did well there,' he said, smiling kindly. 'You'll be one of us yet.'

I couldn't help beaming. How was it that sometimes people at the circus said just the thing you'd been longing all your life to hear?

'Would you like to help Pickie and me with our act? We've got to sort a few things out.'

We found Pickie in the backstage area, and whilst Dickie was checking a few things with him, I walked over to the unicycle. I wanted to try and get on it but didn't want to do so without permission.

Pickie saw me looking at it. 'Do you want to have a go?' he said, with a twinkle. I replied that I did, very much.

'Well, watch how I do it first,' he said. 'The trick is to pedal as soon as you've climbed on it or you'll fall off. You've got to get momentum up right away.'

Pickie sprang on to the unicycle and immediately started cycling. 'Now, if you want to break, then you've got to backpedal. So you go forwards, back a bit, forwards, like this. That way it keeps stable.'

He hopped off and gave the unicycle to Dickie to hold upright. 'Here, I'll need to lift you onto it,' he said. 'First you need to backpedal just a little, then give the biggest push you can to take you forward.'

Soon I was making a wobbly sort of progress around the dusty ground outside the big top. I fell off once or twice but the two clowns made no fuss of me when I did. Falling off was a fact of life and a necessity if you're going to learn, Dickie said. 'You wouldn't be a member of the circus if you didn't have a few scabs and bruises,' he chuckled. 'Wear 'em with pride.'

After that, Dickie and Pickie both looked out for me and took a fatherly interest in my learning. They taught me how to tumble and do a headstand flip. I thought I'd learned some of the basic moves pretty well in the school gym, but the two clowns added a whole new dimension. Loads of new tricks.

'The thing is, Judy,' Dickie said. 'You've got to learn how to breathe and get your energy up. Like this.' He showed me what to do, then I tried again. My flip immediately improved.

'You're a fast little learner,' the clown said. 'And I like the way you're not one to give up easily. Come back when you're older and you can be in my act.'

When Dickie said that to me I felt my cup was full. He probably didn't mean it, but it was still a lovely thing to say.

The time came for our move to Zoo Lake. Everyone was up bright and early, ready for the journey. There was a noticeable buzz of excitement in the air. Even the horses, who would soon find themselves being bumped and rattled along the dusty roads, didn't look unhappy about it.

It was amazing how quickly everything was packed up and put away. It only took half a day. Each person in the circus had a job and Mr Wilkie employed about fifty hands to help. It must have looked like a huge colony of ants that day, with everyone about their business, seemingly without ever needing to be told what to do. And while costumes and props were swiftly stowed in the caravans before being put on the back of trucks, inside the big top us kids were all hard at work too.

We'd been given the job of dismantling the ring. Our first task was to fold up the large piece of matting that covered it. I'd always thought the floor of the ring was covered in sawdust, but now I realized this wasn't the case after all. After the mat was put away we had to stack up the big blocks that formed the ring itself. They had to be in the right order. Like a giant puzzle of tessellated shapes, we knew that if we stacked them wrong we'd find it much slower work when we got to Zoo Lake and had to build the ring again. It was the same with the seats, which we had to pile up in the right number sequence, ready for the hands to carry to the truck.

When we'd finished, the big top was ready to be pulled down. The canvas was suspended by guy ropes from two pillars, and once they were untied everyone waited for a single command to let go of their rope. Then the canvas came down in a rapid whoosh to lie flat while the hands folded it. It only took them minutes and was wonderful to watch.

By early afternoon we were on our way, and as I sat on a box in my little train compartment I was brimful with excitement. I longed to go and stand on the steps at the back of the train and watch the scenery roll away from me like a big, colourful ribbon; but I stayed put, happy enough to be safely stowed away, like one of the props.

I just wished we could keep going and leave the city altogether. Only then would I feel safe.

Chapter Eighteen

*A*fter the big top was put up and all the animals fed and exercised, everyone was exhausted so I didn't get a chance to explore Zoo Lake the first day. When I did, I saw that it was a beautiful spot. A favourite place for pic-nickers, on any weekend in the summer it would be packed with families swimming or sailing. There was a shady bar-becue area under the trees and after lunch, in the heat of the day, people enjoyed walking in the woods around the lake. The place was teeming with birdlife and it made me laugh to see the gangly-legged secretary birds looking like fussy old spinsters with the quills on their heads sticking out at odd angles.

As I walked around the lake with Carl, taking in the sheer beauty of the place, I couldn't help myself wonder-ing if I'd be safe here. Every time the thought surfaced it felt like a cloud had suddenly moved across the sun, and I shivered. At one point I looked down at the little hairs on my arm and saw they were standing up.

Carl noticed my shiver.

'Hey, what's the matter?' he asked. 'You can't be cold, surely.'

'I'm just wondering if I'll be safe here,' I said. 'This is

where half the girls from my school live. I just wish we'd gone to Durban or somewhere.'

I was sorry to have spoiled our walk, but I didn't want to stay by the lake any longer. 'Come on,' I said to Carl. 'Let's get back to the circus.'

At first I was careful not to be seen before the show if I saw families milling about the circus ground; but as the week went by and I got used to my new surroundings, I started to relax. The feeling that there was something horrible lurking just out of sight, ready to pounce if I made a wrong move, started to recede and I just got on with the life of the circus as before. If only I had trusted my instincts and remained on my guard! I should have heeded that snake in the pit of my stomach, which always writhed uneasily when something bad was going to happen. But I didn't.

A couple of weeks went by and I grew happier and healthier with every day that passed. By now, my hair was a tangled bush and the sun had tanned my skin a dark brown. All the circus artists knew me by now, and my confidence was growing in leaps and bounds. It was as if I was a sapling stretching out to the sunshine for the first time.

To my delight, earlier that week I'd been asked by Billy Dash if I could help mind the chimps before the show. I'd leapt at the chance, and Carl said he'd help too. Billy took us to his caravan and opened the door. The chimps were all sitting there, as if they were waiting for us. We dressed them in their little skirts and shorts, and when they put their long wiry arms around my neck it felt so good. I'd never been hugged like that before.

The chimps were never still. If I was trying to dress one of them, she would be pulling my hair while one of the boys stuck his finger in my ear. They were always so playful and loved being out in the ring in the limelight. As soon as the music struck up for their act, they'd know it was their turn to perform and would start squealing and chattering madly. Then, when it was over, they'd clap along with the audience, curling up their top lip as if they were laughing with them. This made the children clap even harder.

They say that you don't always appreciate what you've got until it's gone; but, in my case, I savoured every waking moment at Wilkies. Everything I'd done – everything I'd had done to me before – lay like a dark shadow in my past and the bright, shiny here-and-now was like a gift I unwrapped every single day.

One Saturday afternoon, I was on my way to see the horses when I stopped dead in my tracks. A few family groups were idling around the tents and caravans before the show and I sensed, a moment before I saw anything, that someone was watching me. I was right. A girl was standing stock still, staring in my direction. And I recognized her instantly.

Yvonne Fleming was typical of the sort of girl at Barnato Park school I detested. And here she was now, looking missish in her flouncy skirt, gazing right at me. I knew it couldn't be much worse. Yvonne was a teacher's pet who followed Miss Poole around like a yapping little Pekinese, and she always loved to tell tales. I knew what she'd be spreading around the school first thing on Monday.

Yvonne pulled at her mother's arm to get her attention; she turned and bent her head to listen to what her daughter was saying. Then they both looked at me.

It's started, I thought and the snake writhed its warning inside me.

I walked quickly away to the animal tent and pressed my burning cheek to Lady's neck while she reached round to nuzzle my hand. My heart was beating uncomfortably fast and I felt very sick. *Breathe*, I told myself. *It'll probably be okay. He may not get to hear anything. And he might not bother to come even if he does.*

On the Wednesday of the following week, I was in the animal tent grooming the horses when I saw a tall, familiar figure striding towards me. I felt as if the devil himself was coming for me, and it was as though all the blood had drained from my face and body in a second, leaving my legs feeling like pieces of foam rubber. I couldn't have run if I'd tried.

Behind my dad, Mr Wilkie was hurrying to keep up and I could tell, even from a distance, that he was feeling very uncomfortable, moving rather stiffly, his face redder than usual. Dad must have given him an earful about harbouring an under-age runaway who should have been in school.

I barely flinched when my dad lunged for me, grabbing my arm viciously with one hand while clouting me across the ear with the other fist. Although there was a deafening, throbbing surge of pain, for a brief moment I felt emotionless, shocked into an icy nothingness – almost as if it was happening to someone else. *Here we go again.*

Mr Wilkie ran forward, in an attempt to stop my dad hurting me.

'Please, don't do this. Please … stop!'

My father ignored him and grabbed me by the collar. 'You're coming with me. Now.'

He dragged me out of the tent and I stumbled to keep up with him. I glanced quickly behind me. Mr Wilkie was still standing in the same place with a stricken face.

'Where are your things?' my father asked me. I led him to the train to retrieve my case.

It was only then, as we were leaving the circus ground, that waves of fear and grief hit me – not so much the fear of what was going to happen to me when I got home so much as the heart-stabbing wrench of leaving what, in a short six weeks, had become so very precious to me. And, as with others who'd passed through my life and become dear to me – Miss Williams, Edna, and Gyp – I wasn't given the chance to say goodbye to Carl and the others. And that hurt too.

Dad dragged me by the arm through Braamfontein and down Kotze Street, which ran through Hillbrow, cursing and spitting all the way. He was so angry that I wouldn't have been surprised to see smoke puffing from his nose.

'The trouble you've got me into,' he ranted. 'I had to sell my suit to pay the fine.'

It hadn't occurred to me that truancy officers might come round to check on me, or that my father would be hauled up in front of the school board. *Oh God*, I thought. *If the authorities have been poking into his business, I'm really going to get it now. He'll kill me.*

For a half hour, my dad ranted on at me as he strode and I stumbled through the streets of Johannesburg. I felt like I was being hammered, inch by inch, into the ground, like one of the tent pegs at the circus. *Maybe soon I'll disappear altogether.*

When we got back to our room at the Allendene, Freda was sitting on the bed, looking strained and red-eyed. My dad had obviously been on at her before he'd left, angry that she hadn't been around to report my running away. The board must have given him a real grilling.

Then the battering started, and I wasn't aware of anything else.

I was thrown like a sack of beans from one side of the room to the other, unable to keep my footing and sprawling into furniture until I felt every bit of my body must have been bruised and grazed. Each time my father laid into me with a punch or a kick he yanked me from where I'd fallen and threw me back across the room. At one point, the side of my bed jabbed into my kidneys as I fell backwards against it; another time I went ricocheting, headfirst, into the wardrobe.

Freda got scared then. I think she realized that my dad had gone beyond the point of knowing what he was doing – that he'd been swept up in an animal rage he couldn't control, and that he might kill me.

As soon as she got the chance to slip past my dad and put herself between him and me, she darted across the room and opened the door. 'Get out! Get out and run!' she said, grabbing me and pushing me as hard as she could out of the room.

I was barely able to walk, reeling from the blows to my head, but I didn't need to be told twice. My eyes were a blur, but I managed to stagger down the stairs and out of the hotel into the car park. I made it to a big, black Buick, one of the resident's cars, and climbed onto the back seat. Luckily for me, people rarely locked their cars in those days. I lay down on the padded leather and remained in the same position, motionless, the whole night, feeling the throbbing shock waves pass through my body and pound, like enormous breakers, at my eyes and temples.

I didn't go to school the next day as I was feeling far too sore to venture out of the Allendene. Luckily my dad wasn't around, so I was able to have a bath to ease the bruising and to lie on my bed for most of the day.

When I did go back to school I was faced with a whole barrage of bullying from the teachers. Mrs Langley, the headmistress, positively revelled in holding me up as an example to the school. She asked me to stand up in assembly and showed me off like a head on a spike for people to gawp at. Her message was perfectly plain: *This is not the kind of child we want at Barnato Park.*

As she told the eight hundred pupils sitting in that vast hall what I'd done and where I'd been, everyone gave a smug little shudder. I felt like a character straight out of some Victorian cautionary tale. *Look girls*, Mrs Langley would have liked to say. *If you don't mind your p's and q's, you might end up like this unfortunate piece of dirt.*

Then, at breaktime, a strange thing happened. A girl called Denise came up to me.

'You can sit with us if you like,' she said, indicating where her gaggle of friends were sitting on the wall. 'You know, I think you were really brave to run away to the circus. There are loads of girls here, I bet, who are really jealous. They'd never have the guts to do anything like that.'

I looked at her to see if she was for real – that this wasn't some horrid joke where the next moment they'd all be ganging up on me. But her smile was natural and warm. It was then I realized that I wasn't the only one who'd read *The Circus of Adventure* and dreamed of a life of freedom. In the strait-laced world of Barnato Park, some girls thought that what I'd done was impossibly romantic, and I'd gone up a peg in their estimation as a result.

That day, Denise de la Hunt helped me realize that not all the girls in the school were tarred with the same brush, and that felt good. I found her big, open smile and the direct way she had of looking at you very refreshing after all the snide little sideways glances the girls usually gave me. I don't remember saying much to her that breaktime, but to be included in the group was enormously soothing on a day when I'd felt the full force of the enemy ranged against me. And then, as we walked to the lab for our science lesson, she asked me if I wanted to sit with her.

After that, things might have got better at Barnato Park; but, as it turned out, I wasn't there long enough to find out.

The night my father beat me was a turning point for Freda. She'd had enough. Occasionally, I'd notice that she'd been in to collect some of her stuff, but she no longer stayed at the Allendene. My father stayed away too, finding life much easier, no doubt, with Cherie, his rich divorcee girlfriend. He was clearly sponging off her – I'd noticed some dapper new suits and cravats hanging in the wardrobe, and I reckoned that, as usual, he'd found a willing sucker, happy to be his partner in crime *and* pay for the privilege.

And so I found myself alone in the hotel. After experiencing the noisy hubbub of family life at the circus, having to eat, sleep, wash my clothes and take myself off to school each day on my own felt awful. Added to which, I had a growing sense of unease. Always, in the back of my head, lurked the fear that someone would find out I was fending for myself and have me sent away to a children's home. After the horrors of St Joseph's, I knew I never wanted to experience life in an institution again.

One day, a few weeks earlier, I'd been on my way to some woods near the northern suburbs called the Wilds. I sometimes went for a walk here and would pass what I thought was a private school with a nice-looking playground. It was only when I saw the sign, 'Houghton Children's Home', that I realized it wasn't a posh school at all and, as the realization hit me, I felt my legs instantly turn to jelly. The feeling took me totally by surprise, the trauma surfacing so suddenly, without warning. I thought that if I stood there too long a big arm would reach out and pull me inside.

In my efforts at covering up the fact that Dad and Freda had left, I became quite adept at dodging awkward questions. If one of the residents asked me where my father was I'd tell them that he'd left early for work. Luckily, it never seemed to occur to them to doubt my answer. Before I left for school each day, I was careful to use a bit of Freda's soap and leave some of my dad's clothes lying around. I'd rumple the sheets on their bed, knowing that the maid wouldn't then tell Mr Adams that it hadn't been slept in.

Of course, I thought about going back to the circus; but whenever I did, I soon dismissed the idea. I knew it would only cause Mr Wilkie trouble if I turned up again. I didn't want to go through the awkwardness of his having to tell me to leave if I appeared again, looking for a place to hide. But it wasn't just that. I felt that the stuffing had been knocked out of me after my last bid for freedom and that to escape again would be an impossibility. My dad would only find me and bring me back again, and the next time he really would kill me.

I'd been in South Africa just over six months now and the summer was coming to an end. Soon, I thought wistfully, the circus folk would be heading for their winter quarters at the farm. At school, with the cooling of the weather, most of the other girls were starting to change into their black winter uniforms, and I wondered at what point I'd get into trouble for continuing to wear my white piquet dress. I knew, this time, that there was absolutely no hope of getting anything out of my dad as he still hadn't returned to the hotel.

I got my period for the first time that July. Without any money for towels, I just had to make do with wads of the shiny, hard toilet roll they had in the loos at school. At first, when I saw the blood in my knickers, I thought I must have cut myself somehow. But then, when the bleeding stopped after a couple of days, I put it out of my mind – I had plenty of other things to worry about. It was only when I bled the following month that I put two and two together and realized that this might be a regular thing. And then, a few days after that, I heard a couple of the older girls whispering in the changing room about having the curse and needing a pad, and then the penny dropped. *This is something other girls have too.*

One afternoon, I got back to the Allendene to find Mr Adams waiting for me on the steps. Barring my way so I couldn't pass, he puffed out his stomach, which already protruded quite far between his braces, as if to say, *Don't try to get past me, Missy.*

'I've got a letter here for your father,' he said. 'You'd better make sure he gets it. The rent hasn't been paid for weeks and I'll need to let out the room to someone else if he doesn't pay up.'

I took the letter from him and said I'd give it to my father.

'By the way,' Mr Adams said. 'I don't know what's going on, but before she left, your mother gave me an address where I could get hold of your dad if he wasn't forthcoming with the money. You might as well have it.'

He handed me a piece of paper, on which Freda had scribbled a telephone number and an address. I guessed it was Cherie's as she'd written, 'c/o Mrs Warren'. *How it must have galled her to write that*, I thought.

I waited a couple more days, hoping against hope that my father would turn up; but he didn't. I knew things couldn't just stay as they were, now that Mr Adams was about to give us our marching orders; so I decided there was only one thing for it: I'd have to go to Cherie's apartment. That way, I'd be able to hand my dad the letter and find out what was going on. Not knowing what the future had in store was killing me. I was scared of facing my dad – I hadn't seen him since the beating – but it still felt better going in search of him than sitting at the hotel, helplessly waiting for Mr Adams to kick me out. At least, this way, I felt I was taking some control of the situation.

It took me ages to find Newlyn Mansions. The flat was on the sixth floor at the end of a long corridor. I checked the number on the door and knocked. I couldn't hear any sound inside. I knocked again and again.

Finally, a woman came out of the next door flat. 'It's no use your knocking,' she said. 'Mr and Mrs Petch have gone away to Natal. There's no one there.'

The woman was about to go back inside her flat but stopped when I spoke: 'I'm not sure I'm at the right flat,' I said. 'What does Mr Petch look like?'

'He's tall and thin. Dark. With a little beard.'

Definitely my father.

After Cherie's neighbour had closed the door behind her, I slumped to the floor and sat there for a while feeling sick and hopeless, my back against the door of the empty apartment.

What on earth am I going to do now?

Chapter Nineteen

*M*y situation rapidly became a crisis. I went to Cherie's flat every day, but she and my father were still away. As expected, Mr Adams told me we had to be out of our room within the week and I began to cast around for a plan in earnest. I rejected the idea of telling one of my teachers at school or talking to any of the hotel residents. Either way, it would probably mean a children's home for me, or the most terrible beating from my father. If Mr Wolfe had still been alive I would have told him, but he wasn't and there was no one else I trusted. I always felt safer working things out for myself. Talking to adults only meant one thing – trouble. As I'd always been brutally schooled to keep my mouth shut, doing anything else felt unsafe.

I left the Allendene the following Sunday. I knew the streets would be empty as the African workers were at home in their townships and the majority of whites at church. I got up early and packed my brown school case with just the bare essentials: my school books and uniform, a bar of soap and a comb, a change of clothes, underwear, and a few bits of fruit I'd taken from the hotel dining room. I made sure that I ate a good breakfast before I left as I didn't know where my next meal was coming from.

I slipped out of the hotel and onto the sleepy early-morning streets, walking in the direction of Hillbrow, an upmarket neighbouring district which had plenty of restaurants and hotels. I reckoned that it would be a good area to search for somewhere to sleep as there was a greater likelihood of my being able to scavenge food there.

When I got to Hillbrow, the streets were almost deserted: just a couple of stray dogs and one or two people going about their business. I tried to look as though I knew exactly where I was going so that I wouldn't get stopped by anyone. People might have wondered, otherwise, why a twelve-year-old was out on her own, looking lost and carrying a case.

Most of the backyards in Hillbrow had secure fencing or locked gates, and it took me a good part of the day to find anywhere that might be suitable to spend the night. Eventually, when I was almost ready to give up, I spotted a gap in the wall of an alleyway that led into a yard. Luckily, it wasn't overlooked. On one side of it was the back of a liquor store; facing it was an old shed, which must have once been the servants' quarters. Now it was where the owner of the shop stacked up his crates of empties. I reckoned it would provide as good a home as any.

Inside, the shed smelt of damp earth and stale beer, but it was dry and would give me what I needed. And, as I checked out the yard, I realized my luck was in: there was a water tap against the wall.

Before I made camp in the shed, I thought I'd better check out my immediate neighbourhood. I wanted to make sure I'd worked out my safest entry and exit to the alleyway and where the nearest public toilets were. I found I didn't have too far to go; there were a couple of cinemas close by which I could use in the evening, the Clarendon on Pretoria Street, and the Curzon on Kotze Street; and during the daytime, there was a department store, the OK Bazaars. If I was really stuck, there was always the hospital or the railway station.

There still wasn't a soul around when I came back to the yard. I quickly set to work. First, I rearranged the crates to make a space for me to sleep, making sure that I'd be hidden from sight should anyone come in. I then took my face flannel, wet it, and began wiping down the dirty, cobwebby concrete floor as best I could, going back and forth to the tap to rinse the cloth. When the job was finished I shut the door and sat down on a crate. The small window had been blacked out, which meant I was all at once entombed in thick darkness. I shivered then, and was glad of the sliver of light coming from under the door.

The rest of the afternoon was spent wandering the local streets and watching families out for their Sunday lunch. I didn't know it then, but I was going to hit the point of near starvation in the coming weeks and these open-fronted cafés and restaurants would be a godsend.

It never crossed my mind then that I might have to sleep rough for more than a few days. I was sure my dad would return to Johannesburg soon and that this was simply a temporary arrangement. It was, however, nine months before I once more had a home, nine months of sleeping on a concrete floor, washing in public toilets, and scavenging from bins.

That first night was pretty grim. I hardly slept a wink. I tried to lie down on the floor but insects ran over my body and, without any sort of mattress, the cold soon seeped up into my bones, chilling me stiff. Eventually, I tried to sleep up against the wall with my head against my school jersey, which I'd turned inside out and rolled into a ball. I sat there in the pitch black, feeling alone and terrified and on full alert in case there was a need to run for it. There was no lock on the door and I could hear raucous men's voices in the alley late into the night and the crash of their bottles as they chucked them against the wall.

Please God, don't let them come in here, I prayed silently.

The next day, I was up just before first light, not wanting to spend a moment longer in the shed. I knew I had to be out before the first workers arrived – luckily the first tram of the day went past the bottle store, so I could judge what time it was from that.

I filled a bottle under the tap, making sure that I didn't leave any splash marks on the ground, and took it into the shed. My flannel was no use now so I used a wad of toilet paper to clean myself, taking care to rub behind my ears as Mrs Poole always checked our necks during her dress drill. As I had no toothbrush, I rubbed the paper across my teeth as well. I needed to wash away the sour taste of fear which still lingered in my mouth.

As it was Monday, I knew that it wouldn't be long before the streets were busy with early-bird commuters heading for the city centre; in another couple of hours, kids would be on their way to school. My intention was to keep going to school until the term finished. I knew I'd get my dad into trouble with the authorities if I was a truant again, and that he'd most likely kill me if I did. I realized with a sickening feeling that I was going to find it hard to look anything other than crumpled. With no basin, and only the tap in the yard, my white school dress and socks wouldn't stay white for long.

On my way to school, I thought how strange it was that, while I knew what the other children had in their bags — exercise books, pencil cases and packed lunches — none of them would ever imagine that my case held clothes and a bar of soap. It was hard to see them chatting brightly to their nannies, well-breakfasted and with their sandwiches safely packed away for later.

I was relieved that I only had a few weeks left of school before the start of the holidays. I was concerned, however, that once Barnato Park packed up for the long break I would no longer have my free breaktime snack to live on. Every day we were given a bottle of milk and a piece of fruit, and on Fridays chunks of cold fried fish, which I knew I'd be able to hide in my pockets to keep for later.

When school finished that day, I walked back to Hillbrow and used the afternoon to hunt for something that would make lying on the cold floor of the shed more comfortable. I managed to find some flattened cardboard boxes behind Woolworth's and laid them out to make a mattress of sorts. That night, feeling a little more used to my new home, I slept a bit better.

Every day, I went back to Newlyn Mansions to see if my father and Cherie had returned. As I walked there, I'd be thinking, in rhythm with my steps, *He's going to be there today. He will be there today. He's got to be there today.* But when I got to the flat and knocked on the door there was never any sound. The first week, I was sure he would turn up, find the letter, and go back to the Allendene to check on the situation there; but, as time went on, I began to lose hope.

One afternoon, I went back to the Allendene and looked up at our window from the street. I hoped I might see a sign that someone was staying in the room; but all was quiet, and the window was closed. I skulked on the pavement for a few minutes, under one of the jacaranda trees that lined the street, but didn't dare go inside the hotel. Then, after three weeks, I stopped going to Newlyn Mansions altogether.

Life for me became all about survival: the constant and exhausting search for scraps of food and small change, or for public washrooms to keep myself and my clothes clean. It took every ounce of energy and resourcefulness I could muster to keep going. I had to be constantly on the alert, and there was hardly a moment when adrenalin wasn't coursing through my body.

Only when I lay on the floor of the shed at night, when loneliness clung to my back like a giant black bat in the darkness, did I ever think of anything other than how to survive the next moment, the next hour, the next day. I remembered, back in England, how I used to look at the stars and dream that they were my family, guarding me protectively from afar. But in the shed, my eyes couldn't penetrate the blackness and I felt very alone.

If my mind ever wandered to my mother and sisters, I'd quickly think of something else. I didn't dare to hope or dream. If I had, it would only have been followed by a gut-wrenching ache of disappointment, which I didn't feel I could bear. I needed to be strong and focused to survive. Yearning for a family, or dreaming of a better life, made me weaker, which I couldn't afford to be.

As for getting through the school day in one piece and keeping up with my studies, it was nothing short of a miracle that none of the teachers seemed to notice what was going on. But in South Africa in the 1950s, people would never have believed that a white kid could be living rough. Such a thing was unheard of. Impossible.

I quickly solved the problem of washing my school uniform. I'd realized that the tap in the yard wasn't going to be any good to me as I was so terrified of leaving splashmarks on the earth; nor was there anywhere clean and flat to lay out my dress. I knew it wouldn't look passable for more than a couple of days at most, so I decided to head down to Yeoville's open-air swimming pool to use the showers there. It worked a treat. Although there wasn't any soap, I did nearly as good a job on my dress as I'd managed in our room at the Allendene. My only problem was the lack of an iron.

I took my wet clothes outside and sat down beside the pool. There were lots of kids milling around who'd spread their towels on the ground so no one noticed my dress and knickers, stretched out flat in the sun to dry. I knew that without an iron, my dress would look more crumpled than before, but I hoped I'd get through the school drill in one piece. I folded it carefully, pressing down hard on the material, trying to make it looked like it had been pressed; but the sleeves looked a mess and I knew it probably wouldn't pass.

As the days went by, I got increasingly bold and resourceful. Once I'd given up on my dad coming back, I ventured further into town. If I was going to have to use public toilets, then I decided I'd treat myself to the best as often as I could. And the Coliseum Bioscope's ladies' restroom was pure paradise. It was palatial, with a carpeted floor and sweetly scented little bars of soap on the basins (which quickly disappeared into my bag, along with a toilet roll). There were little bottles of perfume, which I used to dab on my wrists; and, whenever I had a spare penny,

I'd buy a pad from the sanitary towel dispenser. No one used the room while the film was showing, so I had a bit of privacy to wash.

Of course, you couldn't just step off the street and use the toilets at the Coliseum, and getting in there took a bit of nerve. The first time I gave it a go, in my second week of living rough, I was feeling particularly tired and fed up. I was walking along the street listlessly, knowing I had hours to kill before bedtime, when I passed a very grand-looking cinema. Outside it was a poster advertising a Norman Wisdom film, *One Good Turn*. I stood there for a few minutes, looking at the poster and wondering what the film would be about, before deciding I just had to find a way of getting in.

Half way through the first showing of the afternoon I approached the doorman and looked innocently up at him.

'I'm really sorry but I came out at the interval and I've left my ticket inside.'

The man looked back at me sternly. 'You know you can't get back in without a pass-out.'

I didn't budge and continued looking up at him, sensing he would cave in eventually, after he'd got bored of doing his 'big official' act.

'Please, my big brother's inside and he'll be worried about me.'

The doorman gave in at that, moving his body aside to let me past. 'Just this once, then. But I don't want to catch you doing it again.'

Before going in to see the film, I went and checked out the ladies' room. Later, freshly scrubbed and smelling of roses and sitting back in my plush velvet seat under the twinkling stars of the imitation sky ceiling, I cried my eyes out. Norman Wisdom was playing a loveless child, like me, raised in an orphanage and then staying on as an adult to help the kids out of all sorts of scrapes. I couldn't get enough of the film and watched it over again, in tears the whole time.

Once the school term ended, I was relieved that I could pack away my uniform and not to have to pretend any more that everything was normal. But, as the long days became weeks, I felt loneliness settle on me like a lead weight. I had never spoken much, finding silence safer; but now, if anyone asked me anything, I felt barely able to find my voice and the words, when they came, sounded strange to my ears.

I passed some of my time in the library or at the record shop, which was just down the street from the bottle store. It was particularly handy to dive in there when it was raining, and it was a good place to go first thing in the morning. It was a small shop with a counter opposite the door, in front of which were boxes of 78 rpm records, which I'd leaf through before going to sit on one of the chairs against the wall, waiting my turn for the head-phones. We were allowed to listen to three songs.

Sitting on a stool in the booth at the record shop with my eyes closed, listening to a soothing classical symphony or one of Pat Boone's songs, was one of the few times I found I could relax at all. But the feeling was always very short-lived and, as soon as I'd had my turn, one of the restless teenagers waiting in line would move in to take my place, clutching the latest Elvis Presley record.

That summer of 1957, everyone was mad about Elvis the Pelvis, but I preferred the clean-cut, boy-next-door type. Pat Boone was my favourite singer and, when I managed to catch one of his films at the Bioscope, I always found myself wondering whether those carefree high-school days, summer beach holidays and families with big white smiles really existed in real life. I'd certainly never seen people being so nice to each other. *Maybe people in America are actually like that*, I thought to myself.

As it was the school holidays, I used to see a few of the girls from my school in the record shop. They'd always come in with a friend and make an awful lot of noise, giggling and flouncing about in their circular skirts and petticoats. The booth had two sets of headphones so that they could listen to a song at the same time, and they'd sit there, jiggling their legs on their stools, mouthing the words at each other.

I was always ashamed to be seen handing back my three records and never actually buying one. It felt embarrassing, week after week, to have to say the same thing when the shop assistant asked, 'Do you want it?'. Each time I would reply, 'No, no thanks, it's not what I wanted. I'll come back later and listen to another one.'

All through that long hot summer, without my school snack to sustain me, hunger became a ravening wild dog, always at my heels, nipping and growling. What was especially difficult for me was that food was everywhere in Hillbrow and there was no way I could put it out of my mind. In restaurants and street-side cafés; in the mouths of people chewing; or advertised on billboards – everywhere it beckoned to me. Once, while I was walking under some scaffolding where builders were working on a shop refurbishment, I thought I smelled freshly baked bread. In my head I knew it couldn't be and that it must be some sort of varnish the builders were using, but I found I couldn't walk on and had to stand there, rooted to the spot.

Soon I was up to the tricks I'd learned as a toddler combing the bins in Patricroft. I tried looking through the rubbish behind Woolworths and OK Bazaars, but didn't find anything to eat, only boxes and packaging. I discovered the best source of pickings was behind the greengrocer's, where I usually found a few pieces of rotten fruit, carrot tops and the outside leaves of cabbage greens. They were very tough to chew, but I'd gone beyond caring.

Eventually, I got so hungry that I had to pluck up the courage to steal food from a restaurant, although it was a couple more weeks before I dared to take the tip as well. Before I actually made my move, I'd been hanging around, watching and planning, for days. I'd worked out that the open-fronted restaurants along the main streets of Hillbrow would be the safest to grab food from. My best bet, I reckoned, was to wait until a large family were just getting up to go: if there were plenty of kids in the party, then there was sure to be leftovers.

That first Sunday, I hung around nervously outside the Bella Napoli for an hour or so, watching carefully and planning my move. There was a large and noisy family group seated at a table near the pavement. I waited until the moment when the women were starting to feel under their chairs for handbags and the men were getting up from the table to fetch their coats. Then I pounced.

I knew I had to make my move before the waiter came to clear the table – no more than a couple of minutes. During that time, I swiftly tipped bread rolls from their basket and scooped any leftovers from the plates into my carrier bag and darted out of the restaurant before you could count to five. None of the diners took any notice of me. I'm sure they thought that I was one of the Italian kids, helping out in the restaurant.

That first time, I was too nervous to steal the tip, but I soon got bolder. I became lightning-quick at reading a scene – the faces of the customers; when they were about to get up or turn round; when it was safe to swoop in; and the moment I must slip away. But I never let myself become complacent. All it would take, I knew, was one sloppy move and I'd be in big trouble. I was always aware that there might be a policeman about; and, however tempting, I was careful never to steal from the same restaurant twice in the same week.

That first afternoon, I didn't stop to eat immediately but walked down the hill to Joubert Park, where I sat down on my favourite bench. Sometimes, I would sit for hours and watch the weaver birds busily building their huge nests, but today I wasn't aware of anything but the food in my bag. I made myself a *boerewors* sausage and salad roll, which I ate ravenously, not even pausing to pick the bits of tomato and lettuce off my clothes. I longed for a second roll but knew I had to save the rest for the next couple of days, when pickings might be scarce.

Chapter Twenty

I spent many hours in Joubert Park that summer. Without school, I found myself with interminably long days to fill. It wasn't safe to stay in the yard, and I knew I'd get booted out of the record shop or library if I hung around too long. Often I'd take a book out in the morning and spend the whole of the afternoon reading it in the park, returning it before closing time.

My favourite spot was a bench near a giant chess board where the old men of Hillbrow used to gather to watch a game. The players would have to move enormous, child-sized pieces across the board, and I loved to watch their wrinkled, old faces as they paused to ponder their next move.

On the mornings I visited the park, I'd always see the same old woman in a frayed tartan coat and wellingtons walk over to the players and watch their game. She had an equally old-looking dog walking along creakily beside her.

Then, one day, she sat down on the bench beside me and started to talk. It had been weeks since anybody had spoken to me and she startled me at first. I'd begun to think I was invisible, and it was a strange feeling to be noticed.

'You like watching the game too, don't you lovey?' she asked me. I nodded. 'I don't understand the rules, but it's good to see the old boys playing.'

The old lady didn't seem to mind that I wasn't saying anything. Little by little, however, I relaxed enough to ask her a question.

'What's your dog called?'

'My husband Soli gave her the name Bitsy, because he said, "She's just bitsa this and bitsa that".' She let out a wheezy gale of laughter, which made her pause to catch her breath.

'You know the name of my dog now, so I'd better tell you mine. It's Mrs Ezra,' she said. I noticed that her voice had quite a strong accent and that it sounded a bit like Mr Wolfe's. 'What's your name, dearie?'

I told her and she said that it was a pretty name. Then she heaved herself off the bench with a sigh. 'Well, I'd better be on my way or Soli will wonder what's become of me. He's poorly at the moment and I don't like to leave him on his own for too long.'

The next morning in the park, I hoped that Mrs Ezra would come over and sit beside me again and was delighted when she did. This time, she told me all about her family in Durban.

'I hoped you'd be here again today,' she said with a twinkle. 'So I brought you some photographs of my grandchildren to show you.'

She fished an envelope out of her bag. 'Shuffle over, then, dearie.' I moved my bottom along the bench until I was tucked in beside her. I wondered how she could possibly wear a wool coat in the summer; it felt hot even sitting up against it.

As if she'd read my mind, Mrs Ezra smiled and said,

'Old bones. They get cold easily. Do you know, even in the summertime, Soli and I have our fire on most evenings.'

As Mrs Ezra showed me the photographs and told me the story of her family, I had that same feeling of comfort I'd experienced the previous day. It was as if her kindness was being wrapped about me like the softest blanket.

Afterwards, as she pulled herself up from the bench, she asked me if I might help her carry her bag of shopping up the hill to her apartment. I jumped up at once, feeling pleased that she'd asked me.

'Well, that's very kind of you to help an old woman, Judy,' Mrs Ezra said. 'Your mother would be proud of you.'

Mrs Ezra hadn't asked me anything about my home life, for which I was thankful. I sensed that she'd realized I was a lonely child with troubles at home, but she was not the prying sort, even though she must have guessed everything wasn't all right with me. I'm sure she thought I'd open up to her if I wanted to, in time; but until then, she'd let me be.

We walked up the hill slowly to Garth Mansions, where Mr and Mrs Ezra lived. At the front door she asked me if I'd like to come in. 'I'm sure you'd like a cup of coffee and a biscuit,' she said. 'And you can meet Soli. He doesn't get out much these days so it'll be nice for him.'

Inside, the sitting room was warm and stuffy. Mr Ezra was in an old, comfy-looking armchair with his feet up on a stool. He looked very small and frail, sitting there amongst the huge dark pieces of furniture that filled the room. When he spoke to me, his voice sounded reedy and faint.

'Hello, Judy,' he said kindly. 'Now that's very kind of you to help with the shopping. Sit yourself down, Mrs E won't be a moment and then you can tuck in to a biscuit.'

When Mrs Ezra brought in the coffee and biscuits I had to stop myself from stuffing the lot in my mouth. But I hadn't become as desperate as that, yet, and managed to satisfy myself with two, although I'm sure my eyes never once left the plate.

When she saw me to the door, Mrs Ezra looked at me straight in the eyes for a moment and put her hand on my arm. 'Life goes on, dearie,' she said. 'Life goes on.'

It was as if the space between the years had vanished for her and she was looking at some time in her own past when things had been particularly harsh. I understood then why the old lady had approached me when no one else had. She knew when another person was in pain, and had felt drawn to me. Perhaps she saw in me something of the child she had once been.

Mrs Ezra gave me a pair of pink flipflops for Christmas and a little hanky with a 'J' embroidered in the corner. She told me that she was going away the next day to stay with her daughter in Durban. I was glad to have the flipflops. Perhaps people wouldn't think I was homeless if I wore them sometimes. Most of the younger kids in South Africa went barefoot in the summer, but I was very aware that my clothes were looking more and more dirty and the flipflops gave me a bit more confidence.

After Mrs Ezra had left, I felt very alone and no longer liked to sit in the park, knowing I wouldn't meet her and Bitsy there. In the centre of Johannesburg, on Eloff Street, shoppers were rushing about with bags of presents and everywhere I went I heard the jingling of carols proclaiming peace to all men. In the department store, I watched Santa giving presents to the children and thought he must be roasting in his red suit.

The more excited people became as Christmas approached, the more depressed I felt. It really hit me then that everybody was together, busy preparing for an event they were going to share with people they loved. *I'm surrounded by all these people and yet nobody sees me,* I thought to myself, miserably. I felt even worse than I had on the boat the previous Christmas, if that was possible.

I was desperately worried as well. With the shops and restaurants closing for three or four days over Christmas, I wondered how I was going to find any food.

On Christmas Eve, I went back to Cherie's apartment, hoping that Dad might have come back to Johannesburg to preach at Christmas; but there was no sign of life there. As the afternoon wore on, I felt increasingly anxious. I had no plan, and no way of getting food. By the evening, all I could think of doing was following the rest of the families to church for midnight mass. *Maybe,* I thought, *I should to ask the priest to help me.*

St Joseph's hadn't given me a particularly good opinion of priests, but I thought it was worth a try. I went into the church and sat down in a pew. Around me, the place was filling up and there must have been three hundred packed in by the time the service started. I didn't feel at all comfortable surrounded by so many people, and the more panicky I became, the more I thought how hopeless my plan was. *I haven't the nerve to talk to the priest and wouldn't know what to say. Anyway, it would only get me in trouble. If my father finds out I've been blabbing, he'll kill me. Say nothing to no one. Say nothing to no one. That's what he always says.*

I sat there, looking fixedly ahead at the altar, my heart pounding in my chest. Then, as the organist began to play the opening bars of 'Once in Royal David's City' and the choir started to process up the aisle to their stalls,

I stood up quickly and fought my way out of the pew. I was gasping for air.

Outside the church, I stood drinking in the night air and looking up at the stars, just as I had done years before in the nursery at St Joseph's.

That night, in the bottle shed, I came up with a plan at last. I asked myself where families might go for the day if they didn't want to celebrate Christmas in their homes and suddenly I remembered Zoo Lake, which I'd explored with Carl. It was a long way to walk from Hillbrow, but I was certain there would be people there on Christmas Day.

Zoo Lake turned out to be a godsend. It took me a couple of hours to get there but once I'd reached the Northern Suburbs I found that the plane trees that lined the streets made a huge green canopy that protected me from the intense midday heat. Red and purple bougainvillaea blossom tumbled in tangled vines over the wooden *stoeps* and garden walls of the houses. Everywhere it was green, shady and calm.

I was tired and footsore when I arrived at the lake but was immediately cheered to see tendrils of smoke curling up through the trees. As I drew closer, I almost broke into a run as the smell of barbecued sausages reached my nostrils.

I had to wait until the families had finished eating and had dumped their paper plates of chicken bones and salad into the large bins by the picnic site before I moved in. Standing there at the sidelines, trying not to look conspicuous, I knew how a starving jackal must feel, waiting his turn near the carcass, tongue hanging out.

When everyone had gone off to swim or sail their boats after lunch, I went over to the bins. With fingers covered with ketchup and grease, I combed through the rubbish until I had a carrier bag full of meat, bread rolls, and salad. I reckoned I had enough to last three or four days, if I was careful.

And when that runs out there is always the drive-in, I thought to myself.

A couple of weeks before, I'd been exploring downtown Johannesburg when I'd seen a poster advertising a film that was going to be shown at the Top Star Drive-in Bioscope. I didn't really care about seeing *Three Coins in a Fountain*, but it occurred to me that a drive-in might be the perfect place to scavenge for food and coins. And I'd been right.

It was situated on an old mine dump and it took me over an hour to walk there from Hillbrow. The first couple of afternoons, I just stood at the entrance, watching people come and go and working out how I was going to get in for free.

But it was easier to get past the man on the gate than I'd thought. All I had to do was pretend I belonged to one of the carloads of people who had already been through. I'd seen many parents letting their kids out of the car to play on the swings until the film was ready to start, so it was easy to make out I belonged with them. I made sure to memorize the colour and make of one of the larger cars in case I was quizzed by the man on the gate, but he waved me through without a problem.

It was now the Saturday before school was due to start. Before the break, I'd been given a list of the books and sportswear I'd need for the new term. It was hopeless to think I'd be able to go back without them. When I was first living rough I'd gone to Barnato Park every day, fearful that, if I didn't, I'd get beaten to a pulp by my dad for truanting; but now I had far more pressing worries to deal with. My supplies had all but gone.

I decided to make the long trek out to the drive-in with my carrier bag, hoping I'd find some pickings there. As it turned out, it was both a successful and a disastrous evening.

When I got to the entrance, I was waved in as usual. Once inside the enclosure, I picked my way through the small crowd of picnickers until I found what I was looking for. Near the front was a friendly-looking family with an enormous picnic, big enough to feed an army. I guessed they must be on their holidays or they wouldn't have bought so much food.

I went over to the mother and waited until she realized that I was hanging around wanting to speak to her.

'Hello, there,' she said. 'Are you okay?'

I trotted out my well-rehearsed patter. 'I was wondering if it would be all right if I sat with you. Our car's really near the back and I can't see the screen very well.'

'Of course you can!' she said, making a space for me on the rug. 'Come and join us. And you'd better tell me your name.' I did so and then her attention drifted to her little boy. 'Joseph, just one at a time, please! Here, take a napkin.'

A moment later, she remembered me. 'Would you like a drumstick too? We've got plenty to spare. We'll never get through it all.'

I thanked her and took the chicken leg, tucking into it ravenously. The woman looked thoughtfully at me for a moment. 'Goodness, your legs don't look much fatter than that drumstick you're eating! Eat up, my girl.' Then she laughed kindly. 'I bet your mother's always saying that.'

If you only knew. I thought bleakly. *There's probably only three or four people in my whole life who've ever said 'Eat up'.* And then I remembered Miss Williams for a moment, with her tray of fairy cakes.

Everyone went quiet just then as the film was beginning. I wondered if I could reach out and help myself to more food, but didn't feel I should. My mind wasn't on the film at all; it was just circling round and round the plates of chicken and sandwiches.

At half time, the kids' dad put his hand in his pocket and brought out some coins. 'Joseph, Anne,' he beckoned to his children, who were already wandering off to play. 'Would you like an ice cream?'

They skipped over excitedly and he gave them each a few pence. Then his wife spoke to me. 'Would you like one, too?' she asked. 'Hey, Anne, wait on. I'd like you to get one for Judy as well, please.' She gave her daughter another penny.

I'd never had ice cream in a cone before and was thrilled. Anne came back with a large whippy vanilla one with sprinkles on top, like the ones I'd seen people buy at the circus from a machine at the hotdog lady's stand. *What a bit of luck choosing this family*, I thought happily as I licked the dribbles from the side of the cornet.

The film seemed to be going on an awfully long time and before the end I grew restive. I knew I had to get back to the yard before the drunks came into the alley and started kicking up a rumpus. Usually I'd be in my bottle shed by seven, but now I reckoned it must already be past eight.

I got up from the rug and whispered my thanks to the lady beside me. I still had to go on my hunt for coins and didn't want to miss out on the opportunity. I'd quickly found out that if I walked along the rows of cars, searching the ground beneath the drivers' windows, I might find the odd penny or threepenny bit that had been dropped by the waiters who went from car to car offering drinks and peanuts.

And now my luck was in again. I found two tickies – threepenny bits – and a penny.

Afterwards, though, walking through the darkening streets, the glow I'd felt earlier started to fade and, as I made my way along Kotze Street towards my alley, the snake of unease in my belly began its familiar writhing. I'd never got back this late before and knew it wasn't safe here.

I entered the alleyway and saw, to my relief, that all was clear. The drunks hadn't yet arrived. It was only when I slipped through the opening in the wall that led into the yard that I realized I wasn't alone. But by then it was too late to get away. There was a man standing between me and my exit into the alley.

I had the most horrible feeling that I'd been here before, that I knew what was going to happen to me now. And, like that time on the beach at the Isle of Man, I simply froze. I wanted to run and scream but, like in a bad dream, my legs wouldn't move and the breath stuck in my throat. I wasn't in a dream, though, and the man, when he came up close, smelt too strongly of sweat and beer for me ever to suppose I was.

'Wharra you doing here?' he asked me in a slurry voice.

'My . . . my dad works in the shop,' I told him, quite unable to hide the fear in my voice.

'You lying little kaffir,' he said, grabbing me by the hair and twisting my head back so that I was looking straight into his eyes. They were mean.

I realized, when he'd called me a kaffir, that he must have thought, with my dark skin and bushy hair, that I was a black girl. I knew then I was lost.

'Please, please let me go. Let me go! My dad, he works in the shop. He works in the shop!' I couldn't think of anything else to say and felt suddenly like I was going to pee in my pants.

'Shut up, you dirty slut!' he grunted, pulling my face to his and shoving his mouth over mine while he fumbled with his fly with his other hand. 'Come on, come on,' he mumbled. 'Christ, you're a skinny kaffir.'

I tried to fight back but that made him angrier and he punched my face. I couldn't breathe as he had me by the throat. With one of his legs he kicked my feet out from under me, forcing me onto my knees, and I think I must have blacked out because I don't remember anything else.

When I came to, I was lying curled around myself on the dirt floor of the yard. The man had gone and the alley was quiet. I gingerly lifted my head from the ground and drew myself onto my knees. I couldn't yet stand up. Then, trying to take steadier breaths so I wouldn't be sick, I managed to get to my feet and pull up my shorts. Every bit of my body felt bruised and broken and I could feel that I was sticky with blood, on my legs and in my mouth where he must have bitten me; but the terror was still so strong in me that I was galvanized to get out. *I've got to get away, got to get away! He'll come back and kill me. I know he will!*

Everything had fallen out of my carrier bag in the struggle, and so I felt around on the ground to retrieve as much as I could. Then, somehow, I managed to stagger from the yard, down the alley, and out into the street. I don't know how I got to the railway station but I managed it somehow. It was the only place I could think of that would be open all night. If it hadn't been for the fear coursing through my body, I don't think I could have walked at all. But I didn't feel the half of my injuries that night. All I knew was that I couldn't go back to the yard. Not ever.

When I got to the station, I went straight to the ladies' room and locked myself in one of the cubicles. I didn't know if I wanted to retch, pee, or faint, but all three feelings were intense. I was palpitating with fear and sat, collapsed on the toilet, with my head on my knees. I don't know how long I stayed there, but it was a long time.

Later, as I was standing at the basin trying to wash the blood off myself, I caught sight of my face in the mirror. It didn't look like my own. It scared me to see it.

Chapter Twenty-one

*A*fter the attack, I ceased caring what was to become of me. I no longer thought up ways to find food, or bothered to keep myself clean. My head wasn't able to make any plans at all. If I'd been thinking clearly, I would probably have thrown myself under the first bus I saw. Instead, I just moved from hour to hour by some basic instinct. All I knew was that I had to get out of Hillbrow, to somewhere far away from the yard where I'd been raped.

Two days after the attack, I got on a train, without knowing or caring where it was going. My body was moving creakily, like an old woman's, and even managing the step onto the train was agony. I got off at a place called Lenasia and dragged myself along the platform looking for a place to rest. And there I saw, in a deserted railway siding, an old yellow train carriage, rusty and dilapidated.

I climbed aboard, through a door hanging precariously by one hinge, and lay on the metal floor. I didn't go anywhere or move from that position for many hours. Night blended into day and I was aware of nothing except the dark and cold of night-time, followed by the warmth of the sun in the middle of the day. As there were no windows in the carriage, it was like being inside a bean can. All the seats had been ripped from it, leaving metal bars along the floor which I tried to squeeze myself between. But the ridges of the hard steel bore their imprint into my back and legs whilst the cold froze my bones stiff like dead twigs. I'd thrown my school case into an old water butt so I had no school cardigan now to keep me warm or to cushion my head.

Eventually, I had to get up and look for water. I made my way slowly out of the station and onto the dusty road. It was a few hundred yards to the nearest houses, and when I reached them I saw that I was in a place quite different from anything I'd seen before in Johannesburg. They were all painted different colours: yellows, pinks, and blues, a cheery note amidst the wretched poverty of the place. From some of the houses came the sound of a strange jangly music accompanying a high-pitched wobbling kind of singing.

Lenasia, I discovered, was an Asian community, and a world away from Hillbrow. Here there weren't any shops or restaurants, just a smoky warren of dirt roads and tiny bungalows with corrugated iron roofs. It wasn't as stark as Soweto, a township I'd seen from the bus, which was a grey wasteland of tin and mud shacks with no trees or plants, decoration or colour. Here the houses – although basic – were brightly painted, which gave the place a cheerier feel. But I could see it was still very poor and, as I passed by a derelict petrol station, I realized that I hadn't seen a single car on the streets.

With the lack of any food to be had, I nearly perished in Lenasia. I did manage to find water, which, to my shame, I had to drink from the shared toilet at the end of the street nearest to my railway carriage. As I squatted in the little tin shack, which grew to be as hot as an oven by midday, I spotted a little pot with a spout tucked in the corner. When I looked into it I found that it was full of water. Years later, I discovered that keeping clean was an important part of the religion of this community and that the water I drank from the pot's spout, heated to almost boiling point in this cauldron of a tin shack, was used to wash a person's private parts after going to the toilet. My drinking all the water must have caused an agony of irritation for those who lived in that street who found the pot empty every day.

If I hadn't had such easy access to a toilet and drinking water, I wouldn't have stayed in Lenasia at all, and that might have been better for me. As it was, I slowly sank into a listlessness brought on by starvation. I no longer cared what became of me.

I came to Lenasia in late March and stayed there for over two months. At first, I'd forage for scraps every day, choosing to comb a couple of the nearer streets during the quiet interval after people had left for work and the kids had gone to school. I didn't feel strong enough to venture further afield. Sometimes I found a bag containing scraps of food that were completely foreign to me. But most days I had to go without. Any rubbish parcels I did find, I had to fight over with a pack of stray dogs, desperate, thin animals with sharp hackles and ribs that almost poked through their skin. I had to make sure I got to the parcels first before they'd been ripped apart.

Can a human being sink any lower than this? I wondered. *I'm worse off than the stray dogs I find myself fighting with for chicken bones. At least they belong to a pack. I'm alone here and if I die no one will know. Maybe the dogs will fight over my bones too.*

With these macabre thoughts came the most horrible nightmares – strange hallucinations brought on by my starved state – in which monsters chased me and vile slimy creatures with my father's eyes came out of the walls and loomed over my prone body. At some point I'd ceased bothering to go out to look for food at all. Lying there in my steel box, I didn't even register whether it was night or day. And because of the hallucinations I was having, I hardly knew either if I was asleep or awake.

I must have had my thirteenth birthday in Lenasia, but I wasn't aware of its passing. I'd got to a point now when I no longer felt hungry. It was as if I was floating somewhere under the water in a place of half-light, possessed by a deep lethargy, the rhythm of which only varied when the ghoulish waking dreams held me in their grip.

I don't know what made me finally get up. It wasn't as though I really cared what happened to me. I'm not even sure I understood how close to death I was. Now that hunger pangs no longer racked my body, it wasn't something I was aware of any more.

I raised myself slowly, leaning on my elbows, and got to my knees. *Got to go back to the city. Got to wash. Got to get a job. Got to eat.* Stray thoughts floated around my head. I tried to get them into some kind of order, but it was like trying to catch flies in a box.

Without a mirror I couldn't see what sort of state I was in, but I knew I must look a sight. There was blood on my shirt and on my face. I only guessed that it was from a nosebleed from the taste of it in my mouth when I sniffed. I tried running my fingers through my filthy hair, but it was too matted and came out in clumps when I tried. The skin on my hands, feet, and elbows was raw and peeling, and inside my mouth I could feel sore, ulcerous patches with my tongue.

I made my way out of the carriage and onto the street. It took a superhuman effort to put one foot in front of the other, but I made progress nonetheless. It was as if I was on some sort of autopilot. Outside the station was a bus stop and a group of waiting people. When the bus came, I got on with them; when they got off, I got off too. My head was spinning and I managed to walk halfway along a street before realizing that I couldn't see at all. I blinked my eyes for a moment, trying to focus, then my whole body buckled and I collapsed against a shop door and slumped to the ground.

The next thing I knew I was gazing up into a woman's face. She looked concerned and was asking me something in Afrikaans. I couldn't answer her and then she really seemed worried. She went to fetch the shop assistant and together they helped me inside and onto a rest bed in the back room. After I'd drunk a little water, the shop assistant spoke to me:

'Is there anyone we can telephone? Have you got a parent we can contact?'

'We don't have a telephone.'

'Well, if you give me your address we'll go and find your mother.'

I didn't know what to say then. I only had the Newlyn Mansions address, so I gave her that. *They're going to find out now that I'm all alone, that there's nobody living there.*

And then, an hour later, my father arrived.

I remember nothing of the next few weeks: who nursed me or how they did it. I can't imagine Freda or my father feeding me soup from a spoon, or helping me to the bathroom. I think I might have been at Cherie's for a while, before being taken to Freda's flat in Hopkins Street, as I dimly recollect hearing a woman's voice saying 'Let's soak a cloth in vinegar. It might bring the fever down.'

When my fevered head finally cleared of its swarm of muddled sounds and dreams, I found myself lying on a sofa in an unfamiliar room. I was on my own. I dimly remembered being collected by my dad and taken somewhere in a taxi so I guessed that this was where he was living. I was too limp to feel nervous or even curious. It must have been early afternoon as I could hear the noise of children coming home from school. I drifted off to sleep and when I next woke it was early evening. I knew immediately I wasn't alone in the room.

'Oh, you're awake.' Freda's cold tones made me tense up inside as instantly and involuntarily as a mollusc reacts to an unpleasant invader.

I hadn't seen Freda for about ten months. When we were sharing living space at the Allendene I'd hardened myself against those knee-jerk feelings of trauma which always threatened to throw me around like a puppet. I hadn't exactly grown inured to her malice but had found a way of blocking it out. It hadn't been so hard as she'd hardly been around and, when she was, she mostly ignored me. Now though, unprepared as I was, I couldn't protect my soft underbelly quickly enough. Just seeing Freda's pinched, hateful face was like being thrown across the room by a sharp cut to the solar plexus. I felt violently sick.

When my father came home, much later that evening, I had retreated to a state of weakness, caring about nothing, so seeing him didn't have much effect on me. Like Freda, he barely looked at me. At one point she had brought me a cup of soup and a slice of bread but beyond that gesture, it was as if I wasn't there.

For the next three months, from June to September, I lay on Freda's sofa recuperating. I had no choice but to help myself to eggs and bread from the kitchen and borrow

Freda's soap when I bathed, though I was always nervous about doing so. Sometimes I dipped my finger in her bottle of shampoo or jar of face cream, but I was always careful to wipe any drips or stickiness from the rim afterwards.

I didn't know why Freda had taken Dad back, or why she put up with me in her flat. It wasn't as though my father was any nicer to her. He was still spending the day-time with Cherie and would talk to her on the telephone in the hall every evening after he'd come in. Presumably, for form's sake, Cherie hadn't wanted him to move into Newlyn Mansions with her, so Dad had tracked down Freda to provide him with a bed.

In spite of everything, Freda still felt some attraction to my father and wanted to see if she could win him back. I watched her vain attempts to try and look attractive and fashionable, but nothing ever looked right on her. She'd changed the way she did her hair, from the tight curls and Kirby grips, which women had worn in our Manchester neighbourhood, to an even less becoming backcombed style. She'd tried to go blonde but the dye had made her dark hair turn a nasty mustard colour, and the hair was so thin that you could see her scalp through the puffed-up beehive on top. Worse still was how badly the style suited her sharp, sulky face. I didn't wonder that my dad barely looked at her when he came in.

'How was your day?' she'd say.

'So-so,' was the only response she got.

My dad was particularly jumpy in the flat at Hopkins Street. It can't have just been that he was penned in with Freda and me. There was definitely something else both-ering him. I wondered if the school board had been on his tail again, otherwise he wouldn't have asked Freda to put me up. But I sensed that he had other, bigger worries.

He paced up and down the apartment, and would check the post nervously. He peered through the glass doors in the lounge at the street below any time he heard a noise outside. Whenever I could, I escaped to the balcony and let Freda and him have the room to themselves.

Little by little, from muttered phone conversations and the odd thing he let slip to Freda, I picked up what Dad was up to. It was more than a year since the closure of the Triangle Band Healing Sanctuary, after which he'd been hissed off the platform at one of his Spiritualist events. Realizing that they had been supporting a con man with a tendency to seduce the more vulnerable members of the congregation, the Spiritualist church in Johannesburg had banned him from preaching. Never one to feel shame or sit licking his wounds for long, Dad was soon cooking up new business schemes with Cherie.

One of these was a 'spiritual postal service', which involved placing advertisements in the local papers. There was no shortage of lonely old ladies, lovelorn spinsters, or bereaved people who'd willingly send postal orders to my father. In return, he'd send them a taped message from a departed loved one, or a personal horoscope. I hated to see my father prey on these sad, vulnerable people.

It was the beginning of summer by the time I was well enough to leave the flat. It had been a difficult few months. I felt so powerless and weak, and at the mercy of Freda and my father's moods. Neither of them ever hit me now — maybe they thought I was too big at thirteen for that — but it was hard sharing a living space with two people who never so much as looked at me. They hadn't once asked where I'd been living for the nine months I'd been sleeping rough. I think each presumed I'd been living with the other. Anyone else would have shown some curiosity, however unfeeling; but Dad and Freda almost enjoyed demonstrating that they had absolutely no interest in me. It made me horribly on edge; and although there was some respite when they both left for work, I soon felt my stomach tensing again, waiting for their return each evening.

With a great deal of grumbling, my father forked out for a school uniform and exercise books, ready for the new term. It felt very strange going back to Barnato Park; but although I was nervous about it, something inside me had changed since being confined to the flat all those weeks. I'd had a lot of time to think.

I'd never run away from my father and Freda when I was very young – I hadn't known where to run to, since I didn't know where my mother lived; and, anyway, I was so terrified of being caught by my dad. Later, once Mum had made contact, she never actually asked me to come back to live with her. Now I realized I was old enough to take responsibility. There was no one else in this but me. I could see a way out, and I was determined to make my way back to my mother and sisters again.

I knew that if I was to have a future which didn't involve staying with my father or living on the streets, then I'd need to work hard at school and find a part-time job to earn some money. I made a pledge to myself that, at seventeen, I would pass Standard Seven with honours, and that on the day I left school I'd throw my hat into the nearest dustbin.

I'm going to get through this and I'm going to show them that I'm not the loser they think. I'll make something of my life and help other kids like me, if I can.

This was going to take some doing. I'd now lost a year and had been kept down in the same class. I was still banned by Miss Schmidt from attending Afrikaans lessons, which was a big problem. Without that subject, I couldn't pass my exams; but I was determined to find a way around that. It's strange how everything is possible when you know what your goals are and have the single-mindedness to reach them.

In my first week back at school I went downtown to the public library and asked the librarian which books I'd need to teach myself Afrikaans. She looked at me kindly. 'You might be interested in this,' she said, handing me a leaflet. 'There's a free tuition scheme available for immigrants wanting to learn Afrikaans. It'll be much easier than learning it from a book.'

I was in luck. Soon I was having a lesson every week and made quick progress. I was diligent with my school-work as well, spending hours on the balcony of the flat, catching up on what I'd missed.

Something else happened that summer to make me all the more determined to earn my independence. A letter from my mother arrived. How it reached me, I don't know, but I suppose my dad must have kept Mum's solicitor informed of where he was living.

In her letter, Mum asked me how I was and told me how my sisters were doing at school. 'I often wonder how you're getting on in South Africa and how much you've grown,' she wrote. 'It must be very different from Manchester. I expect you're as brown as a nut with all that sun. I wish we could have a bit of it here.'

And she wrote that she missed me.

As I held Mum's letter, hope flared up brightly, and I felt warm inside.

Chapter Twenty-two

For the next three years, I worked as hard as I could. Soon after my fourteenth birthday, I managed to get a Saturday job on the sweet counter at the OK Bazaars. It paid badly, but it was a start. Shortly after that, I got another job at a dairy on the main street in Yeoville, working an early-morning shift before school.

Every day, before dawn, the African nannies would travel into Johannesburg and stop off at the dairy on their way to work to pick up the babies' milk. I had to be there by half past five to serve them. Wearing a pinafore over my school clothes, I stood at the counter for the next two hours, carefully counting eggs into brown paper bags. If one broke, the money would be docked from my pay, and I hated that. Every penny I earned I hid in a sock, which I kept under the sofa. Counting my savings, shilling by shilling, was my one real pleasure. Losing even a penny of it hurt.

It would never have occurred to me to spend my money on records and clothes like the other girls of my age. I had other plans.

Soon after I got the job at the dairy, I walked into the travel agency on Commissioner Street and went up to the counter. A smallish man with thinning hair looked at me with interest, obviously wondering what a fourteen-year-old was doing on her own in his shop.

'Hello, can I help you?'

'I want to buy a ticket to England,' I replied. 'Can you let me know how much the cheapest fare would be?'

'Well, let me see.' He took a file from the shelf behind him and leafed through it for a moment. 'The cheapest way of getting there will be by boat and that'll set you back a hundred and twenty pounds.'

I put a pound down on the counter and the man looked at it without expression. I thought it was to his credit that he didn't react as he might have done, with a raised eyebrow or a patronizing smile. He showed me the same formal courtesy he would have offered any other customer.

'I'd like to leave that as a deposit,' I told him.

'I hope you don't mind me asking, but aren't you a bit young to be travelling on your own?' he asked.

I decided, as he'd treated me well, that I'd let him into my plans. 'I want to go to England to live with my mother,' I said. 'And I don't yet have a passport and I won't be able to go before I'm seventeen when I finish school. I realize that.'

'Well, that's okay then.' He nodded his head, satisfied with my explanation. 'By seventeen, you'll be old enough to travel on your own and all you'll need is your birth certificate and a photograph and you'll be able to send off for a passport yourself. That shouldn't be a problem.'

'So you'll take my pound?' I asked him.

'Of course I will. I'd be happy to.'

With that he opened a big accounts book and turned to a fresh page at the back. 'Here we are. Let's log it in then. What's your name?'

'Judy Richardson.'

'There we go, Judy. One pound.' And he entered the date. 'I'm Mr Harvey, by the way. Delighted to be of service. Just let me know if there's anything else I can do for you. You only have to ask.'

Every week, on a Saturday morning, for the next two years, I visited Mr Harvey's travel agency and put my money on the counter. Little by little, in a quiet, reserved sort of way, we became firm friends.

As soon as he spotted me at the door, Mr Harvey would fill two cups he had ready on the counter with coffee. I always felt warmed by this gesture as I knew it meant he'd been looking forward to my visit. Then, as I sat perched on a stool sipping my coffee, Mr Harvey turned to the big colour map on the wall behind him and showed me how far my latest pound would take me on my six thousand mile journey, moving the drawing pin he used as a marker a fraction closer to England each time.

'Ah now, Judy, we've cause for celebration this week. You've just crossed the Equator.'

By the time I was seventeen, I was working so hard that I barely saw my father and Freda. I'd got a well-paid job at the Regent Cinema in Kensington after a tip-off by the manager of the Gem, a local fleapit, who lived below our flat in Hopkins Street. He knew the manager at the Regent and said he'd heard he needed part-time staff.

At first, I covered Saturday matinees and Sunday evenings, but after a few months I was asked if I wanted to do a couple of nights a week as well. The pay was good and I was given travelling expenses on top, which I always saved, although it was quite a distance to walk from Yeoville. I gave up my job at the OK Bazaars because it clashed with the matinee, and I soon chucked in the dairy too, finding that getting my homework done was becoming impossible. Instead, I cleaned shoes and worked in the kitchens of a local hotel a few hours here and there. By now, I was squirrelling away one pound ten a week.

In my last term at Barnato Park, before school broke up in December, I was told that I had passed Standard Seven with Honours. I could hardly believe I'd done it at last. After all the homework, the extra classes, and the hours in our local library slogging away, it felt really, really good.

As I walked up to collect my certificate from Mrs Langley in assembly, I couldn't resist sneaking a glance at Miss Schmidt.

You see, you mean-eyed old spinster, I managed to do it without you. I'm not such a stupid dunce after all, am I?

I hoped my stare managed to convey all the ill-will I'd ever carried for her. I reckon it must have done as she didn't manage to hold my gaze and was the first to turn away. I felt about ten feet tall.

I achieved another thing on my list of goals that week when I tossed my hat into the bin outside the school gates.

At about that time, I came across an advertisement in a local newspaper for a cheap charter flight to England. Instead of the hundred and twenty pounds a berth on the *Windsor Castle* was going to cost, it seemed I could fly for just sixty pounds. By now, I'd saved sixty-six pounds.

The next day I went to see Mr Harvey and showed him the advertisement.

'Do you think I'd be able to cancel my berth on the ship?' I asked him.

'Let me find out for you. I'll certainly do what I can. Come and see me tomorrow and I'll let you know how

I got on. And I'll see if the June flight's still available too.'

The next day Mr Harvey was all smiles when he greeted me.

'It's absolutely fine and I've reserved you the flight.'

I was so overwhelmed that I couldn't speak. I had to sit down on the stool by the counter for a moment to recover.

'Now, if you haven't done it already, you're going to need to get your passport organized.'

Mr Harvey went on to tell me where to go to have my photograph taken and how to get to the passport office.

The next day, in the flat, I sneaked a look inside my dad's brown case, in which he kept his personal papers. I don't know what I'd have done if I hadn't found my birth certificate amongst them; but, to my relief, it was there. What took me by surprise was the strong wave of disappointment I felt when I read my father's name on it.

All those years of reading books about foundlings who turned out to be princesses had left their mark on me. I'd always hoped that my father was just some wicked imposter. Now I knew for certain it was only a fantasy.

I wrote to tell my mother I was coming, and when my train would be arriving at Euston. Over the past two years, I'd had three or four letters from her and she'd always written that she was missing me. Now, a month or so before I was due to fly, I had a reply from her, saying that Dora would meet me under the station clock.

A few days before I left, I went down to the travel office to pick up my ticket and say goodbye to Mr Harvey. It turned out to be an emotional moment, which took us both a little by surprise.

As I watched Mr Harvey leafing through his file for my itinerary, eyes a little brighter than usual, I thought, *How strange it is that he seemed such a buttoned-up sort of person at our first meeting. I never guessed then what a kind and generous friend he'd turn out to be.*

'Well, I must say I'm proud of you, Judy,' Mr Harvey said a little gruffly. 'I don't think many youngsters of your age would have stuck with it for the past three years. I'm really happy for you.'

I thanked him for being so kind to me.

'Oh, not at all, not at all!' He brushed my words aside. 'But do send me a postcard from Buckingham Palace, won't you?'

I assured him I would.

There was now just one more thing I had to do.

I'd left it until the night before my flight before telling my dad that I was going. He'd just come off the phone to Cherie and was toasting his toes by the one-bar electric fire.

I went over to stand in front of him.

'I've got something to tell you.'

He looked up from his paper, frowning.

I was amazed how I was able to stand there without fear. My knees weren't trembling, and I could even look him straight in the eye. I realized with relief that all I felt now was indifference.

There's nothing at all you can do to me. I've got my ticket, my passport, and money of my own. I'm free of you now.

'I'm leaving tomorrow. I've got a ticket on a flight to England and I'm going to live with Mum.'

'What do you want to do that for?'

I shrugged. I wasn't about to share my thoughts with him.

When Dad saw he wasn't going to get an answer he gave a snort of scornful amusement. He had a way of looking at me pityingly, as though I was the village idiot.

I really didn't care.

You're the sad old git, Dad, sitting there in your socks. Still pretending to be Christ Almighty. I've got my whole life ahead of me. And I'm going where I'm wanted.

I knew it would pique my father that I was going to join Mum. He'd hate to think of us talking about him behind his back. knowing I'd be letting on that he was living in a sad little flat and having to sponge off Freda, and that he hadn't made it as a big shot spiritual leader with a chain of sanctuaries after all.

Before he left for work the next day, my father thrust six pounds into my hand. 'Give it to your mother,' he said.

I nearly fell off my perch. He was usually so tight with his money, and I'd never seen him actually volunteering any. It was painfully obvious that he still needed to show Mum he had the upper hand after all these years.

Chapter Twenty-three

 I arrived at Euston Station and made my way to the big clock.

It had been four days since I'd left Johannesburg and I'd been hopping in little rattle-bone planes all over Africa and Europe since then. My journey had begun with a train bound for Lourenço Marques that took a day and a night. From there, we climbed on board a tiny aircraft, bound for Lisbon, which had to land every two hours to refuel. After a night in Lisbon, we flew to Paris and this morning I'd finally arrived at Gatwick.

Nothing that happened on that journey had the power to dampen my spirits, even when I had to share a bed in Lisbon with a tiresome old lady who plopped her false teeth into my glass of water. When I felt tired, cramped, or bored, I found it easy to switch off at any time to embroider the fantasy that I'd cherished for so many months now.

I'm walking up the platform and making my way to the clock. Before I reach it, I see Dora, blonde hair gleaming and looking so happy, smiling and waving at me. 'Judy, Judy! It really is you!'

Daydreaming had never before felt so delicious. After all, it was the first time in my life something really was going to come good. Something I'd planned. Worked hard for.

I reached the clock and realized I'd made pretty good time. I'd been hoping that Dora wouldn't have had to wait more than a quarter of an hour at most, and it was almost a relief to find she hadn't yet arrived when I got there. I was a bit disappointed not to live out my daydream with a lot of waving and calling but, then again, at least Dora hadn't been put to any trouble. I laid down my bag and stood for a while, feeling excited and a little self-conscious.

Three hours later, sitting on my duffle bag, I had almost run out of possible scenarios to explain Dora's non-appearance. *Maybe her train's been delayed? Maybe she felt ill and couldn't make the journey? Maybe she heard my mum wrong and thinks it's tomorrow? Maybe she's just walking into the station now? Maybe that's her in the pale blue coat? Yes! That could be Dora!*

By late afternoon, I realized that I couldn't just sit there forever, watching and waiting. I knew that Dora and I were meant to be crossing London to Liverpool Street station and to catch a train to Manchester, so I decided that I'd better make the journey on my own.

Before I left Euston, I went up to a policeman and asked him if he'd be on duty the rest of the evening.

'You see, I'm waiting for my sister, who's meant to be meeting me here under the clock. But I've decided to catch the train to Manchester on my own as it's getting late.'

'Don't worry, pet. I'll look out for her for you. If I see a girl waiting here, I'll let her know where you've gone.'

I thanked the man and made my way to the taxi rank. Just over an hour later, I was sitting safely aboard a train bound for Manchester. The earlier setback hadn't dampened my excitement one bit and I wanted to shout at the other passengers: *Guess where I'm going? I'm away! I'm free!*

I hadn't realized how late it would be when the train finally pulled into Manchester's Piccadilly Station. I had no idea how far it was from London. I kept peering through the carriage window to check the station names every time the train came to a halt and couldn't believe how many there were, or how far we'd come. It was almost midnight by the time we got there.

I must have looked as uncertain as I felt, standing alone on the platform, not knowing where to go. Luckily, the train driver spotted me and came over to see if I needed any help.

'Where are you going, love?'

'I need to get to a place called Sale. Is it far from here?'

'Well, it's a bit of a way but I think you're probably in time for the last bus.' He looked at me kindly. 'Come on, I'll show you where to go. We'll get you there, don't you worry.'

The man carried my bag and led me to the bus station. We only just made it. The driver had already started the engine, ready to go, and I climbed quickly aboard. While I sat down in a seat at the front, the man had a word with the bus driver and then turned to me.

'Which road in Sale did you say you needed to get to?'

I told him and the bus driver said he'd let me know when I needed to get off.

The journey seemed interminable as the bus wound its way through suburb after suburb of near-empty streets, but finally the driver called out, 'Norris Road. Here you are, love.'

I was dropped at the bottom of Norris Road. My mother and sisters lived at 419, so I found myself with quite a walk. Along both sides there were council houses, set back from the road with long, ribbon-like, front gardens. I couldn't see the numbers above the doors from the pavement, so each time I wanted to check which house number I'd reached I had to walk all the way up the path to the front door. By the time I reached my mother's house I felt like I couldn't walk another step.

It was dark inside number 419. I knocked, quite tentatively at first, then louder. Then, when no one came to the door, the thought occurred to me: *Of course, they're probably all in bed.* So I looked through the letterbox and then walked round the side passage, rapped on the back door and looked up at the upstairs windows. All dark. The thought came to me then that maybe they were out. I stood there a moment longer, wondering what to do next; then I spotted the coal shed and opened the door to see if I could camp out in there. There was a large heap of coal inside. *There's no way I can sleep on that. What on earth am I going to do?*

I went round to the front again. As I did so, I heard a noise. It was the clink of milk bottles. Next door, I saw a woman in her dressing gown putting her empty bottles out on the step.

'Excuse me, please!' I had to stop her before she went inside again and my voice came out in a yelp.

'Goodness me!' she said. 'You startled me there. Who are you?'

'I'm looking for Mrs Doyle,' I told her. 'I'm her daughter.' I quickly crossed the patch of lawn to her front door.

The woman immediately looked concerned. 'Oh love, they've gone away on holiday. There's no one there.'

I didn't know what to say.

'Look, you'd better come inside. You can stay the night at mine.'

'They said they'd be here. I don't understand.' The thoughts were all confused in my head. *They'd gone away?*

'Look, love, we'll track down your sister, Dora, in the morning. I know where she lives, and I don't think your mum said she was going with them.' She didn't say it, but I could tell the woman was feeling cross with Mum.

Mum's neighbour, Mrs Fazakerley, led me through a passageway to her kitchen, where she gave me a glass of water. I sat down, feeling dizzy with exhaustion and confusion, and drank it while she went upstairs. She came down again after a few minutes, carrying a sleeping child, which she tucked up under a blanket on the settee in the front room.

'Peggy won't mind,' she said. 'They sleep like a log at her age. I think you look like you need a bed tonight.'

I didn't deny it.

I slept deeply that night and woke in the morning feeling much better. When I opened my eyes, I didn't know where I was at first. It was strange finding myself in a room filled with cuddly toys and little girl things. I lay there, not wanting to move, my limbs sluggish with sleep.

Mrs Fazakerley opened my door a few minutes later and brought me a cup of tea, which she placed on the bedside table. 'Don't hurry,' she said. 'I've left the cornflakes out so you can help yourself as soon as you're ready. The good news is that I've managed to get Dora on the telephone and she's coming round as soon as she can. She said she'll take you down to your mum's.'

'Did she say where they'd gone?' I asked her.

'They're at their holiday chalet in Wales. I don't think it's too far.' She paused and gave an indignant little huff. 'I must say, although I know it's none of my business, the whole thing seems very thoughtless, especially as how you've had such a long journey.'

Mum had told me in one of her letters that she had a share in Dad's brother's holiday place in Prestatyn. *But why was she there now?* It didn't make any sense to me. Without any explanation from my family, I couldn't feel disappointment or anger, or even agree with Mrs Fazakerley that my mum was thoughtless. I just felt bemused. *There's bound to be some explanation. She couldn't have forgotten about me. Not after her letters.*

Dora arrived an hour later, looking extremely fed up. She was very different to how I'd imagined her – an enlarged version of how she was at thirteen – and I was utterly unprepared for the efficient-looking, sophisticated nineteen-year-old who turned up. She swished irritably into Mrs Fazakerley's house, wearing a short red cloak and high heels, her blonde hair held up in a French pleat. I thought she wouldn't have looked out of place in a Hollywood film.

I felt suddenly extremely shy and at a loss for words. Mrs Fazakerley made up for it though – she didn't seem in awe of Dora, not one bit. In fact, I rather think she would have liked to have called her a stuck-up little madam. No love lost there.

Dora barely looked at me. Instead, she turned her annoyance on Mrs Fazakerley. 'I had no idea at all that she was coming, so it's no good looking at me like that.'

'Well, I honestly don't know what Judy would have done last night all on her own if I hadn't been around.'

'She wasn't expected as far as I know. Mum said nothing about it.' Dora, still frowning, gave a tight smile. 'Anyway, thanks for doing your bit.'

My sister then turned to me. It was the first time she'd done so. 'Come on, Judy, you'd better get your stuff.'

I felt more stiff and awkward by the minute, as if my bones were all put together at funny angles. I didn't know what to say or how to behave with this cool stranger. The chatty, exuberant welcome – the kisses and hugs I'd been dreaming of getting – had not materialized. In place of the bubbly, tender sister of my dreams I now found myself in the charge of an extremely annoyed person who looked at me as if I were something unpleasant that had to be sorted out. *A visitor you weren't expecting, didn't want to see, but had to do something about. A headache.*

Before we left, I found my voice and quietly thanked Mrs Fazakerley for being so kind to me. She looked at me rather pityingly and laid her hand for a moment on my back, as if to say, '*Poor duck. You didn't deserve this. I only hope you find the Doyle family was worth coming over for.*' I could read her thoughts, but was very glad she didn't voice them. I wasn't ready to hear that from anyone.

I was still hoping Mum would be pleased to see me, and that thought was worth holding onto. But, with Dora's cold welcome, I couldn't help but feel some of my excitement leak out of me, as though someone had handed me a party balloon which turned out to have a slow puncture.

Later that morning, as Dora and I sat together on the train in silence, I remembered how it was on the bus when she used to take me to Mum's. She clearly didn't feel the slightest need to be polite, make small talk, or show any curiosity whatsoever in the sister she hadn't seen for years, and who'd gone missing at the age of two. She'd been too young to remember anything much, and had probably blanked out those traumatic months anyway. Now I sensed she had other fish to fry, wanted to look forward, not back. It was understandable, if things hadn't been easy growing up in the Doyle household.

When I asked about Mary, Dora gave a little snort.

'She's gone to Australia. She's lucky to have got out of this dump.'

My heart sank. I'd really been hoping to see her.

We lapsed into silence again and Dora chewed the skin around her thumbnail, careful not to damage the polish. Then she burst out in irritation.

'I mean, for God's sake, why can't the woman take responsibility for anything?'

'Who?'

'Mum, of course. It's just so bloody typical of her. She never once mentioned you were coming, and yet I'm the one that gets landed in it.'

'But she said you'd be meeting me at Euston under the clock. She wrote a letter specially to tell me.'

'She lives in cloud-cuckoo-land. And she's always burying her head in the sand when something turns up she can't deal with.'

That hurt. *She can't deal with me?* I didn't want to believe it, but my gut told me that what Dora had said was probably true.

'Just don't expect her to come rescuing you on a silver cloud or anything. Most of the time it's been shit for her, and for the rest of us.'

I felt like telling Dora that it hadn't exactly been a bed of roses with Dad, but I kept my mouth shut. We didn't need a double load of whinging in this conversation. Anyway, I wanted to find out more from her if I could.

'In what way?' I asked.

'Oh God, you don't want to know!' She gave the dry snort again. It made her sound like a much older woman, one who'd had a lifetime of shit to deal with.

'Look, you can find out for yourself. But let's just say that Paddy hasn't exactly been easy.'

I remembered my mother's nervousness around him when I'd visited her before.

'Where is he now? Will he be in Wales when we get there?'

'No. He's got a job out in Ghana. Mum gets the odd bit of cash in the post, but it's not enough. Still, it's probably better than him pouring it down his throat here.'

After that, we were silent again until the end of the journey. We sat there, the two of us, sisters and strangers, one chewing her finger, the other her lip.

I hadn't been prepared for how very fat my mother had grown in the years since I'd last seen her. She looked like Humpty Dumpty, almost as wide as she was tall. She was wearing a blue overall and I was reminded for a moment of Mrs Craddock, our neighbour in Patricroft. Huge, snugly bosoms covered in nylon. But that's where the comparison ended. Mum held out her arms when she saw me, saying, 'Ah, come here.' But she was as stiff as a board and clearly felt awkward hugging me.

You're putting on an act, I can tell. You didn't want to believe I was really coming. Dora was right. You just put your head under the bedclothes and wished it would all go away.

Dora had the grace not to have a row with Mum in front of me, but she was obviously steaming. She looked at me and shrugged, as if to say, 'What's the point?'

'Look, I'd better be going. I've missed a shoot today because of this mess and I'll need to get back so I can work tomorrow.' Dora didn't even bother to take off her cloak.

'Dora's a photographer's model,' Mum said to me. 'She's inherited the looks in this family.'

I could tell my mother was thinking of herself, how she'd been when she first met Dad – a girl with the talent to be a concert-hall singer; a looker.

'Right, the girls are already in bed. You'd better be off, Dora. Thanks for bringing Judy down.'

Dora shot my mother a dark look and gave a resigned shrug.

I was relieved that she and Mum didn't have an argument about who was meant to be meeting my train. It would have been embarrassing and I sensed it would have only made horribly plain what was pretty obvious anyway – that my family didn't want me.

Let's face it. Mum only wrote that she was missing me with the safety of six thousand miles of water between us.

She never imagined for a moment that I'd actually turn up on her doorstep asking her to prove it.

Chapter Twenty-four

Things went from bad to worse. We stayed two days in the chalet, which was no bigger than a caravan, with barely room enough for the four of us. Rose and Lily, who at thirteen and fifteen weren't at all happy having an unknown sister foisted on them, looked at me with suspicious eyes over their breakfast bowls. I'd had to share Lily's bed the night before, which hadn't pleased her at all. Neither of my half-sisters remembered me from before; and, as my mother clearly hadn't mentioned me over the years, I must have come as an unwelcome shock to the pair of them.

Back in Sale, Lily went into a huff. I didn't really blame her. She'd been told she had to continue sharing a bed with me and she was furious.

'But Mum, she kicks and I get too hot. Please. I don't want to!'

'Look, Lily, I haven't got the energy for this.' Mum looked exasperated. 'Just do it, okay?'

I had slipped out of the room but I could still hear them arguing, and it made me squirm.

The next morning it was no different.

'But, Mum! Pickles won't sleep on my bed with Judy

sharing it. You said I could have her on my bed! I can't sleep without her.'

Pickles was Lily's first love, a fluffy tabby who spent much of her time asleep in my sister's bedroom.

We lasted two more nights before my mother caved in and I was moved out of Lily's room to sleep on the settee. After that, both my sisters pretty much ignored me.

The day after we got back to Sale, Mum took me down to the Social Security office. At the counter, she spoke to the lady in a whinging, hard-done-by voice. 'I've got no money to look after her. My husband's away in Ghana and I just can't cope with another mouth to feed.'

'I really don't know how long I'm going to be able to look after you, Judy,' she said as we made our way home on the bus. 'It's nice having you and all, but money doesn't grow on trees.'

I'd grown sick of hearing about money not growing on trees the whole time at my father's and it depressed me hearing my mum say it now.

I'd already given Mum the six pounds from Dad, which she'd stuffed in a jar on the shelf, saying, 'Oh very big of him, I'm sure.' His patronizing gesture hadn't been lost on her either. But now, even with the money to tide her over, all she did was complain that she couldn't cope.

As the days passed, I found there were other things that felt horribly familiar too.

I'd been hoping that I could relax at Mum's and have a normal life, in a place where I was accepted; where I could open up and be myself. I longed to be able to pop down to the corner shop and have a chinwag with the lady behind the counter, or chat to our neighbour over the fence – to have an ordinary, comfortable family existence.

It came as a shock to realize that I was Mum's shameful little secret. She'd never told her friends or neighbours that she had another daughter, and now she clearly felt too awkward to explain. She'd no doubt told people I was just a visiting relative, and now didn't want anyone to discover she'd lied to them. At this time, and in this place, keeping up a decent front was all-important, the first commandment. If you didn't, there'd only be nasty tittle-tattle, or people might turn their backs and ignore you when you went down the shops.

During the first week of my stay, I walked into the living room to find that Rose had invited a couple of friends over. I introduced myself to them. 'Hello, I'm Judy, Rose's sister.'

It felt like I'd committed the most shameful treason. I could tell I'd said the wrong thing when I saw my mum's frozen expression. Then, clearly not knowing what to say when two surprised faces turned in her direction, my mother walked quickly out of the room. I stood in the doorway, mortified. I wanted to creep away and hide but I didn't have a bed I could curl up on and Mum was in the kitchen. I went and sat on the toilet instead.

How can I be in a place where they have to hide who I am? Where my mum feels ashamed that I exist? Where my sisters can't stand the sight of me?

I knew then, as I sat there trying to make sense of things, that I was on my own again, and that I'd have to move on soon. It would be a couple more weeks, though, before I knew for certain that it wouldn't be a case of Mum coming to love me the more she got to know me.

During those two weeks, things got worse and worse. Mum started picking on me, at first only mildly but later more viciously, until I didn't know what to do or where to put myself. Everything I did was wrong. If I tried to be helpful, I got ticked off for getting in the way.

Soon, there seemed to be a whole campaign waged against me by Mum and my sisters. I didn't know if they'd actually planned a strategy to get me out – to make it so unpleasant for me that I'd have to leave – but it certainly felt like it.

Nothing was said overtly but I overheard whispered snipings where Rose or Lily would accuse me of borrowing their clothes or touching things in their bedrooms. I couldn't bear the little looks and nudges they gave each other constantly and my mum never chose to stick up for me. She just joined in the assault.

'Judy, there was a pen and a pad of paper in the kitchen drawer. Please don't take things that don't belong to you. Money doesn't grow on trees here, you know.'

She sounded horribly like Freda, who always used to accuse me of stealing her stuff, and it made me want to put my hands over my ears.

The straw that broke the camel's back wasn't long in coming. One afternoon, in my third week, my mum accused me of stealing some photographs. Soon after I'd arrived in Sale, I'd asked her if she had any pictures of me and Dora and Mary when we were little. She'd said that she'd look them out for me, but had never got around to it. Now, two weeks later, she came to me, absolutely furious.

'You've stolen the photos. I know you have, so it's no use lying.'

'But I've never seen them. How could I have stolen them?'

'I know exactly where they were and they're not there now.'

'They must be somewhere else. Mum, please! I really haven't seen them.'

She went off on a rant then, making so little sense that it wasn't worth arguing with her. Her face was a mottled beetroot colour and the bulges of fat around her chin wobbled as she shouted at me. Her eyes didn't seem to see me at all. I stood there, cheeks flaming, horrified she should be saying such poisonous things and wanting her to stop.

'I've got friends in South Africa, you know. They'll find out for me where the photos are. Where you've sent them.'

Stop! Please, stop! I wanted to scream. Somehow, hearing Mum's torrent of petty, ridiculous words – utterly lacking in logic – was the biggest trial of all for me. I just didn't want to be part of it, part of her, any more.

What am I doing here? I've escaped one unbearable life. All I wanted was a fresh start, but I've come back to find this.

I left the next morning while Mum was at the shops. I couldn't bring myself to say goodbye, so I left a note on the mantelpiece instead: 'You've always been a family and I haven't been part of it. I think it's best if I leave you to get on with it.'

I didn't know where I was going to go but I'd seen advertisements pinned to a board in the local newsagent's window. I hoped I'd find someone who had a room to let. Luckily, I still had just over a pound in my purse, though that wasn't going to last long.

I found a grotty room in a house in Crumpsel. I took it because it was cheap, but there were no sheets on the bed, and I didn't have a towel either. At night, I laid my coat over me to keep warm, and during the day I sat with it wrapped around my shoulders. I couldn't afford to buy coal for the fire and, as I was used to the warmth of South Africa, the damp weather quickly stole into my bones until I felt cramped and stiff. I sat in a dismal slump for days, barely moving. Only once did I leave the room, to buy a packet of biscuits from the corner shop.

I felt worse than I ever had before. Throughout all the years of abuse and loneliness one thought had always sustained me: that I'd one day be reunited with my sisters. Now I no longer had that dream to comfort me or spur me on.

What's the point of going on? Why fight for something better when all you get is the crap kicked back in your face? I'm sick of other people. Sod them all.

Like before, in Lenasia, I was filled with a deep sense of isolation, and the haunting thought kept circling around my head: *No one knows I'm here. I'm all alone on this godforsaken planet with no one to care for and no one to care for me.*

I don't know how many days I sat there with my coat around me, hardly moving. I felt like I was sinking further and further down a huge, black hole. I didn't want to do anything or go anywhere. I vaguely heard people coming and going in the boarding house but wasn't aware of much else. Once, when I looked around the room, in my stupefied state the hideous red flowers on the wallpaper seemed to be laughing at me.

After what must have been about a week, something made me claw my way back out of the black hole of depression that had almost consumed me. It was as if I could just make out a pinhole of light far above me, and I struggled towards it, fighting for air. Then, from somewhere inside me, came a voice, an energy that was my spirit: 'You've got two choices. You can either die here or you can go out and start again. You've done it before; you did it on the street. You can't say you don't know how.'

I got a job in Woolworths, on the cotton and button counter. It didn't pay much but I could get a two-course meal in the canteen for a shilling, which helped enormously.

I'd reached a turning point, sitting there in my dismal room at the boarding house, staring at the packet of biscuits which had been my only source of food. Woolworths was just a start, to get me back on my feet, and put a hot meal inside me every day. Soon, I was thinking of finding a better job, and somewhere better to live.

I was scouring the local paper on my lunch break one day when an advertisement caught my eye.

WANTED: Girl with gymnastic abilities to train as trapeze artist. Previous experience not essential.

Chapter Twenty-five

I spoke to a man called Speedy Barham on the phone. He told me that he owned a trapeze act called the Australian Air Aces and that he needed a new trapeze artist to make up part of his team. I told him a little about myself and he invited me to come up to Bellevue for an interview the next day.

I'd seen plenty of posters advertising the Bellevue zoo and amusement park, but I had no idea of the sheer scale of the place. My bus seemed to snake its way for miles around the perimeter of the grounds before eventually dropping me outside the main entrance.

I walked inside and was almost whirled away by the loud hurdy gurdy music coming from a waltzer to my left. Towering over the scene was a rollercoaster, the famous Bobs, with its little carts thundering down the track. The noise of screaming, music and shouting was hugely exhilarating and the colours of the stalls, flags and bunting all flowed into one big joyous tapestry.

I made my way to the circus building, where Speedy had told me to meet him, and my heart started beating faster, not with nerves so much as excitement. It was as if a drumbeat was beckoning me home. I was back at the circus, and every part of me felt it was where I belonged.

I sat down in the huge hall and Speedy joined me a few minutes later. He gave a big, open smile and I felt instantly relaxed with him.

'Hello, you must be Judy,' he said, shaking my hand. 'Let's go to a quieter place and then you can tell me all about yourself.'

Speedy led the way to one of the rooms alongside the main hall. I only realized then, as I followed him, that he was quite a small man. He was the sort of person that had so much easygoing confidence that it somehow made him seem much bigger.

It was lucky that Speedy was so easy in his skin as it made the interview less of a strain on me. I simply answered his questions briefly and honestly. Speedy wanted to know where I'd come from, what abilities I thought I had, and what gave me the idea that I would want to be a trapeze artist.

I told him about Wilkies and what I'd learned there. I sensed that he was pleased I wasn't simply a competent high-school gymnast but someone with a real knowledge of what circus life was all about.

'You know, this act is really hard on you,' he said. 'It's not just about being athletic. Even carrying the gear is exhausting. I'll need someone with stamina and spirit. Only the strong survive.'

Speedy looked at me speculatively and paused for a moment. I gazed right back at him and my expression didn't waver. He nodded then, satisfied.

I'm used to tough. I'm stronger than you'd imagine. A survivor.

Speedy had spoken the language of my life, and it didn't faze me one bit. If I'd managed to lug Freda's big tin bath of laundry at the age of eight, then I'd certainly manage this.

'Righto, Judy,' Speedy got up from his chair and I stood up too. 'I'll give you a week's trial. I'll know by the end of that time whether you'll be a goer or not.'

I wanted to leap onto the trapeze right there in the circus hall to show Speedy what I could do.

I'd got my chance and I was determined not to blow it.

As soon as I got home I spoke to my supervisor at Woolworths and asked if I could take a week's holiday. He said I could and, two days later, I returned to Bellevue.

Speedy's yard was just a short distance from the Bellevue grounds. He opened the big wooden gates to let me in and led me to his tour bus. It was parked next to a large garage building which served as Speedy's rehearsal studio.

The bus was an old-fashioned vehicle from the 1940s, cream, with a big radiator grill. On the door someone had painted what I guessed must be the emblem of the Australian Air Aces: two kangaroos on motorbikes, with a trapeze between them.

I followed Speedy onto the bus and he showed me my living space. I would be sharing the front compartment with the other trapeze artist, Bobby, but for now she was living at home with her mum so I'd have it all to myself. Just behind the driver's seat was a little stove, a cupboard containing cans of food, a table and two chairs. Behind that, was a pair of bunk beds and a wardrobe. Very small, very simple, and just perfect.

'Vicky, my wife – who you'll meet later – shares the back end of the bus with me while we're on tour. I hope you won't get too lonely on your own at night, but it's perfectly safe here. Help yourself to all the food you need.'

I assured him it would suit me perfectly.

'I'm used to being on my own.'

That first day we worked from morning till night, until every muscle, bone and sinew in my body ached. Speedy explained that rehearsals were always tougher than the real act.

'You see, you've got to do it static,' he said. 'Here you have to dangle from the trapeze and have nothing but sheer muscle power to get you out of a trick. There won't be any momentum to help. By the end of the week I'll know if you've got what it takes. And, if you have, the act will seem like a breeze after that.'

Speedy had only five weeks to train up a new trapeze artist for a big event at Bellevue, on Firework Island, that was already being advertised. I hardly dared hope that person might be me – I wasn't exactly used to things going right in my life. But I knew I'd try my hardest, even if it killed me.

Speedy gave me some soft boots and I wore a pair of stretchy trousers, which I knew would be fine for gymnastic work. Then it was down to business.

After warming up, I performed some exercises for Speedy on the bar. When he was satisfied, he asked me to get down.

'Now, Judy, I want to test your arm strength with the wrist straps.'

The trapeze was about fifteen feet above the floor. Speedy told me how to sit on it, then positioned himself underneath so that he could catch me if I fell. For the next twenty minutes or so he took me through a series of moves to get me used to them.

'Right.' Speedy said. 'Now we'll try the Eagle.'

The Eagle was one of my moves in the act. I had to hang by the feet from the trapeze before pulling myself up and through it. Speedy was watching me intently, ready to catch me if my ankles weren't strong enough to hold me.

'Right, let's try it again. This time I'm going to count. You've got to learn to do it in exactly eight seconds for the act.'

I tried it again, and then went on to a series of other moves. My arms were almost shaking from the unaccustomed effort of carrying my body weight.

After we'd finished on the trapeze, and I was almost ready to drop with fatigue, Speedy decided that the time had come to test my strength still further. He took me over to the stack of tracks and other gear that the team had to winch onto the roof of the bus and transport to every new venue, where they built it up into a massive steel construction that would carry the motorbike and the rest of the team on a chassis above the track.

'The tracks are really heavy and awkward to carry,' he said. 'It's essential we can all manage to lift the gear while we're on tour. So let's see how you get on with it.'

Speedy asked me to carry each of the four pieces of track back and forth from the bus to the garage building. After hours on the trapeze, I thought my arms were going to fall off, but I gritted my teeth with determination.

Come on, girl, you managed Freda's bathtub, I told myself. *You can carry four measly bits of track.*

Speedy looked pleased when I'd finished. 'I expect you'll be well ready to put your feet up,' he chuckled. 'You've done well, Judy.'

If my face hadn't already been flushed from carrying the gear, Speedy would have seen it blaze scarlet with pleasure.

That evening, I barely had the energy to open a can of beans and sausages before collapsing on the bottom bunk. Seconds later, I was dead to the world.

The next day, Speedy took me through more exercises. At noon, we broke off for half an hour and met Vicky at the Bellevue café for lunch. I munched on a pork pie while she looked me over critically.

'You're very thin,' she said dubiously. 'I can't believe you've got the strength in those skinny little arms to carry your weight. I reckon you need a bit of feeding up.'

I looked at Vicky in her leopard-skin top. Her shoulders were much broader than mine, and she was pretty chunky.

'Still,' she said, smiling. 'Speedy said you're stronger than you look. Not one to give up easily.'

In the afternoon, Speedy helped me learn all the tricks in sequence. He explained what everyone's moves would be, what Vicky and Bobby would be doing at their end of the chassis, and which stunts he'd be performing on his motorbike along the track below. He counted the beats like a human metronome and made revving sounds to mark the progress of the bike to help me get the timing right. And I performed the tricks over and over again.

'That's not right! Do it again … That's still not fast enough. Do it again.' By the time I came down off the trapeze, my head was aching from the strain of having to concentrate so hard.

While we sat having a cup of tea, I marvelled at the way Speedy would give me instructions. He never acted like a schoolteacher, issuing orders without giving you an explanation or any opportunity of working things out for yourself. Only when he saw I was putting myself at risk would he break in with an instruction.

'You'd better not put your wrists in the straps that way or you'll break your arm.'

I loved being taught by Speedy.

By the end of the week I knew every trick inside out. I had memorized each cue by heart, and Speedy had made me recite his own instructions back at him as I moved about the trapeze. I knew exactly what he and the girls would be doing at any given moment in the act and the importance of getting the timing right. If I was even a beat too slow, Bobby and Vicky might bang their heads or Speedy's bike could come off the track. Everything had to run like clockwork, or one of the team would be put at risk.

Every evening that trial week, once Speedy had gone home and I had time to myself, I hadn't been able to prevent myself thinking, *I just want to live like this ... Want to be here ... Want to be in the act ... Be on the bus.*

And then always the reflection: *But, hey, life hasn't exactly shown me that you ever get what you wish for.*

On the Friday, after we'd finished and I'd packed my bag to go home, Speedy asked me if I could come back the following day to meet Bobby.

'We'll be at the circus canteen at twelve if that suits?'

I told him that suited me just fine.

I didn't know what to expect the next day. When I got to the circus building I found Speedy, Vicky, and a girl with blonde hair, who I guessed must be Bobby, sitting at a table. They were obviously in the midst of a serious discussion. When he saw me, Speedy stood up and pulled out a chair.

'Sit yourself down, Judy.'

I perched on the chair and he went on without a pause. 'We'd all like to welcome you to be the fourth member of our trapeze act.'

I nearly fell off my chair. Had I heard Speedy right? Was he really speaking to me?

It didn't matter that I was at a loss for words. The others all spoke at once in a torrent of excited voices. 'Welcome, Judy!' … 'Speedy's told me so much about you!' … 'Well done!'

I couldn't eat or drink anything that lunchtime. I think I was simply too full of happiness.

That night, and the whole of the following day, I was walking on air. Letting the truth sink in and savouring it.

I'm actually going to be one of the Australian Air Aces. Me! Judy!

On the Monday, I told my landlady I was leaving and gave in my notice at Woolworths. By noon, I was making my way back to Bellevue on the bus with my suitcase.

Early the next morning, we loaded up the tour bus with everything we needed for the show, winching the track and trapeze gear onto the roof. By nightfall we were set up on Firework Island, the construction all finished with its loop of motorcycle track and the big triangular chassis from which the trapeze artist (me) and the aerial performers (Vicky and Bobby) would be suspended.

A small ferry took the bus across to the island, which was surrounded by a moat of water. Firework Island was constructed in such a way that it was set deeper than the ground that surrounded it on the other side of the water. This meant that there was a sizeable bank of grass that encircled it, forming a decent-sized amphitheatre for spectators. I was thrilled to find that we were sharing the island with the zoo animals; and when Speedy parked the bus behind a bank of bushes near their cages I knew I wouldn't feel lonely that night.

And I didn't.

After Speedy, Vicky, and Bobby had left, I heated up some soup on the stove and sat eating it on the steps of the bus, looking out at the sky as darkness fell. I felt a kind of contentment I'd never known before. I'd been briefly happy at Wilkies, but the feeling had always been tainted by the fear that my dad might find me. Here, with Speedy and the others, I finally felt a quietness inside, like I'd come home at last.

I looked up at the stars and remembered how I used to think they were beckoning me to them. Their long-lost child. I felt a tiny pang of loss for a moment, knowing that those twinkling imaginary friends I'd clung to through my childhood didn't feel real to me now. And then the feeling passed. *I don't need you any more!*

I was so used to the huge, black tide of fear and misery engulfing me at the thought of being alone and unloved that I was almost surprised not to feel so much as a ripple disturb me now. Instead, here I was, purring sleepily like a well-fed cat. *What is happening to me?*

After washing up my soup bowl and undressing, I lay down on my bunk and pulled a sheet over me. The night was warm and the air smelled of hay and manure. I could hear the sound of yawns and grunts coming from the animal cages.

A family isn't necessarily what you're born with, I reflected as I drifted into sleep. *You can find it for yourself. So long as you have somewhere safe and warm where you feel that you belong.*

I can see Speedy beneath me, roaring along the track. We're all spinning round, lit up brightly against the night sky, and the sheer force of the wind almost knocks the breath from my body. I have six seconds to move into position and let go. I don't look down but I know the ground's far, far beneath me.

One, two, three, four, five, six.

My hands leave the trapeze and I'm flying. With nothing but my ankles to prevent me from falling. But I'm not going to fall because I'm an eagle. And I can hear, through the wind and the noise of the engine, the roaring of ten thousand spectators.

About the Author

*I*n 1991, thirty years after Judy had been living on the streets of South Africa, Judy's husband died, leaving her a small legacy. A few days later Judy saw a television programme about the troubled lives of children in the townships of South Africa. It was as if a switch had flicked in her.

Within weeks she was on her way to South Africa, having galvanized her family and local community into action to help make the project a reality. Her first trip to South Africa lasted six weeks and within that short space of time she set up community projects to help local street children in the violent townships of Soweto, Alexandra and Sebokeng. The Pegasus Children's Trust was born.

Over the next four years Judy divided her time between fundraising in Great Britain and consolidating her work in South Africa. She also helped set up another centre in a squatter camp outside Cape Town called Khayelitsha. These centres didn't just seek to meet the children's basic food, shelter and clothing needs. With the help of educators that she hired and trained locally, she used drama therapy to help the children come to terms with their often traumatic experiences and to find greater self-worth and purpose. She also organized classes to help them learn to read and write, and encouraged them to develop local craft skills and take part in community fund-raising projects.

The projects thrived and were so successful that Judy went to Mexico to work on similar projects in the slums of Mexico City, Puebla and Oaxaca. Then in 2003 Judy returned to South Africa, this time to Hillbrow where she herself had lived on the streets as a child.

As Judy found with all the other centres she had set up, the problems the children were dealing with were far more complex than the troubles she had experienced: they weren't just sleeping rough, vulnerable to abuse or in danger of starvation; gang fighting, drugs, pimps, AIDS and the sheer number of street children made their situation much more dangerous.

Today Judy still works tirelessly to keep her centres flourishing. When she is not in South Africa helping her co-workers she is fundraising in Great Britain. For more information about Judy, Pegasus Children's Trust and her work in South Africa visit www.streetkid.co.uk.

Pegasus Children's Trust

For information on Pegasus Children's Trust and how you can help please visit www.streetkid.co.uk or write to:

Pegasus Children's Trust
PO Box 5711
118A Bruce Gardens
Inverness
IV1 9AN
Scotland

Email: kidsinflight@tiscali.co.uk

Justcharen.
* Charlie Wilson
feat. fantasia
I wanna be your man